ECONOMIC ISSUES, PROBLEMS AND PERSPECTIVES

PUBLIC DEBT, FINANCIAL DEVELOPMENT AND ECONOMIC GROWTH

ECONOMIC ISSUES, PROBLEMS AND PERSPECTIVES

Additional books in this series can be found on Nova's website under the Series tab.

Additional e-books in this series can be found on Nova's website under the e-book tab.

GLOBAL ECONOMIC STUDIES

Additional books in this series can be found on Nova's website under the Series tab.

Additional e-books in this series can be found on Nova's website under the e-book tab.

ECONOMIC ISSUES, PROBLEMS AND PERSPECTIVES

PUBLIC DEBT, FINANCIAL DEVELOPMENT AND ECONOMIC GROWTH

NATIA KUTIVADZE

NOVINKA

New York

For permission to use material from this book please contact us:
Telephone 631-231-7269; Fax 631-231-8175
Web Site: http://www.novapublishers.com

Additional color graphics may be available in the e-book version of this book.

Library of Congress Cataloging-in-Publication Data

Public debt, financial development and economic growth / editor, Natia Kutivadze (Ph.D. in Economics, University of Milan, Italy) and Senior Analyst at Transparency International Georgia, Tbilisi, Georgia).
pages cm
Includes index.
ISBN: 978-1-62417-980-8 (soft cover)
1. Debts, Public. 2. Financial institutions--Investments. 3. Economic development. I. Kutivadze, Natia.
HJ8015.P8298 2013
338.9--dc23 2013001525

Published by Nova Science Publishers, Inc. † New York

CONTENTS

PREFACE

The goal of every nation's economic policy is to ensure a high and stable level of economic growth. The importance of a financial system in promoting economic growth and reducing poverty has been demonstrated by a number of empirical studies. It is also well known that a country's public borrowing and its nature are important determinants of its economic performance. Moreover, the broader economic consequences of public debt buildups is a topic that is receiving substantial attention in academic and policy circles. Such analysis becomes even more relevant in light of the recent meltdown of the world financial system followed by the incidence of public debt. This book investigates the relationship between public debt composition, financial development, and economic growth by controlling the macro and institutional factors in which the debt was issued in countries grouped by income levels. Different features of these issues and their mutual implications are examined through the application of empirical and theoretical approaches.

INTRODUCTION

The goal of every nation's economic policy is to ensure a high and stable level of economic growth. The importance of a financial system in promoting economic growth and reducing poverty has been demonstrated by a number of empirical studies[1]. It is also well known that a country's public borrowing and its nature are important determinants of its economic performance. Moreover, the broader economic consequences of public debt buildups is a topic that is receiving substantial attention in academic and policy circles. Such analysis becomes even more relevant in light of the recent meltdown of the world financial system followed by the incidence of public debt. In this book, we investigate the relationship between public debt composition, financial development, and economic growth by controlling for the macro and institutional factors in which the debt was issued in countries grouped by income levels. Different features of these issues and their mutual implications are examined in subsequent chapters through the application of empirical and theoretical approaches.

Debt and growth have been connected in the literature in two different ways. On the positive side, government debt can play an important role in growth, for instance, by raising funds for long-term development projects in physical infrastructure and human capital. Compared to other forms of budgetary finance, market-based domestic borrowing is seen to contribute more to: macroeconomic stability (low inflation and reduced vulnerability to external real and domestic monetary shocks), domestic savings, and private investment. Indeed, public debt can support a financial system in credit

---

[1] King and Levine (1993), Rajan and Zingales (1998), Levine (1999, 2003, 2005), DemirgüÇ-Kunt, A. and R. Levine (2001), Greenwood and Jovanovic (1990), etc.

intermediation, or can act as a substitute for it. At times, it can even help the financial system survive crises.

In contrast, excessive public debt can have long-term negative consequences. For instance, a most proposed channel for the public debt-growth connection relates to the extent to which heavy public debt burdens or debt service are likely to have significant negative implications on capital accumulation and reduce ("crowd out") investment necessary for productivity growth which, in all probability, results in the slowdown of economic growth. However, although a growing body of recent literature tries to uncover the relationship between public debt and economic growth, there are no compelling answers to the questions: How does debt accumulation interact with growth? To what extent and under what conditions can public debt be an impediment to growth? What is the growth impact of domestic versus external financing? In the first chapter, we address these questions by providing new evidence regarding the debt-growth nexus across different subsets of countries. Our analysis distinguishes between the growth impact of domestic versus external public debt to examine the importance of domestic financing as compared to external financing for the period of 1990 to 2007. The empirical analysis supports a non-linear relationship between total public debt and growth in the subsets of middle and low-income countries. This relationship is mainly driven by the non-linear relationship that exists between public external debt and growth, and not by the domestic component of debt. Otherwise stated, it appears that high levels of external public debt are associated with low per capita GDP growth rates, whereas high levels of domestic public debt do not necessarily affect growth. We identify ranges of values for the optimal level of public debt (i.e. the level after which the marginal impact of further debt accumulation becomes harmful for growth) in middle and low-income countries. In a subset of high income countries, we did not find any support for a robust relationship between public debt and growth. Another noteworthy result that emerged is a strong link between financial development and growth across a subset of middle-income countries. Our analysis shows that debt structure is relevant to growth and highlights the importance of the development of the domestic bond markets to promote long-lasting economic growth.

Once a strong link between financial development and economic growth had been identified, and the relevance of the debt structure and the development of the domestic bond markets to promote long-lasting economic growth revealed, in the second chapter, we focus on the nexus between financial development and public debt structure (domestic versus external debt). How do domestic debt markets interact with financial development? What is the impact of institutional factors on the development of domestic bond markets for countries at diverse stages of development? These are questions we try to answer through the application of panel data analysis.

Our results provide strong evidence that financial sector development plays a key role in the development of the domestic bonds market which, in turn, supports the issuance of more local currency debt instruments. At the same time, financial development and choice of debt instruments tend to be contingent on macroeconomic stability. Another possible interpretation revealed from our analysis is that, with financial development, a constituency against inflation (proxy of macroeconomic stability) will be established. These findings are consistent with the idea that financial development is greater where constituency favors financial development and rejects inflation. They also support the hypothesis that, in a given group of countries, a more developed banking sector offers the possibility of issuing more domestic debt. Or, the mere existence of a banking sector in a particular country supports financial development as well as anti-inflation policy.

To make the above line of reasoning even clearer, the third chapter is devoted to the analysis of the link among inflation, domestic financial markets, and public debt management. Low inflation may be necessary for financial development, which is crucial in creating a domestic debt market. But, once financial markets are developed, they may also create a pledge against inflation.

Throughout history, however, one of the channels of outstanding debt reduction available to policymakers appears to be associated with a burst in inflation or with a combination of governments' austerity plans and a steady dose of inflation. The literature on the inflationary-bias problem suggests that the role of contractual arrangements, like indexation[2] and, conversely, the set-up of institutional arrangements, like central-bank independence[3], are the ways to limit the inflationary pressures in society. Although, the importance of the intertemporal dimension of the relationship between the policymaker and the private agents has been highlighted and suggested that building up an anti-inflationary reputation may help reduce the inflationary-bias[4]. Diverging from the conventional literature, it has been argued[5], that the political approach to monetary policy provides a better account for deriving institutional solutions

[2] Back and Musgrave, 1941; Lucas and Stokey, 1983; Calvo, 1988; etc.
[3] Rogoff, 1985; Alesina and Gatti, 1995; Walsh, 1995; etc.
[4] Barro and Gordon, 1983.
[5] Chari, Kehoe and Prescott, 1989; McCallum, 1997 and Piga, 2000.

to this bias. Particular attention is also given to the implications of public debt[6] and to its composition[7].

Our approach, which is related to political models, instead stresses the role of a country's financial institution development in promoting domestic versus external debt instruments and reducing the government's temptation to inflate. Institutional framework versus debt management is the key feature of our model of sovereign borrowing. In our model, the government faces two inflation-related incentives. As in a traditional Barro-Gordon model, the government has an incentive to inflate the nominal debt away in order to reduce the burden of distortionary conventional taxation and, additionally, the government has an incentive to exploit redistribution effects of monetary policy.

We show that, in financially less-developed and under-productive economies, when redistribution effects are unimportant, the government finds it optimal to issue inflation-indexed debt (or foreign currency debt) to reduce the inflationary-bias. Conversely, in more efficient systems (which allow banks to be more leveraged and redistribution becomes an important source of financing productive investment), the government issues domestic debt and lowers inflation in states of nature when productivity is high in order to redistribute wealth in favor of banks, thereby enhancing investment and growth. Diverging from the conventional wisdom, our findings suggest that it is the development of the banking sectors that leads to lower inflation and not the other way around. Hence, the model suggests some intuition as to why financial development, i.e. an efficient banking sector, is instrumental to the creation of a domestic bond market and why such development is associated with lower equilibrium inflation.

While this quick outlook of the work makes apparent the importance of the topics addressed in this thesis for the growth potential of modern economies, further investigations are also necessary, as these issues are crucially interconnected. Financial development, public debt management, and inflationary-bias are distinctive features of policymaking, which should be jointly analyzed to fully answer still open questions and to enhance the growth maximizing potential of public policy. This is a task for future research and the focus of my future research agenda.

[6] Cukierman, 1994; Beetsma and Bovenberg, 1997.

[7] Falcetti and Missale, 2002

Keywords: Public debt, Public debt management, Domestic debt, Financial Development, Economic Growth

JEL Classification: C33, E31, G20, H63, O11, O40

Chapter 1

THE IMPACT OF PUBLIC DEBT STRUCTURE ON ECONOMIC GROWTH

ABSTRACT

This chapter[1] examines the effect of public debt on growth by controlling for the institutional environment in which the debt was issued in countries grouped by income levels for the period of 1990 to 2007. Our analysis distinguishes between the growth impact of domestic versus external public debt to examine the importance of domestic financing as compared to external financing. In particular, the regressions' outcome points clearly in the direction of a non-linear relationship between total public debt and growth in the subsets of middle and low-income countries, and this relationship is mainly driven by the non-linear relationship that exists between public external debt and growth, and not by the domestic component of it. Otherwise stated, it appears that high levels of external public debt are associated with low per capita GDP growth rates, but that high levels of domestic public debt are not necessarily associated with low growth. We identify ranges of values for the optimal level of public debt (i.e. the level after which the marginal impact of further debt accumulation becomes harmful for growth) in middle and low-income countries. In a subset of high income countries, we did not find any support for a robust relationship between public debt and growth.

Another noteworthy insight that emerges is a strong link between financial development and growth across a subset of middle-income countries. Our analysis shows that the debt structure is relevant to growth

[1] I thank the participants of the seminar held at the University of Milan (Ph.D. student seminar, December 2010) for helpful comments and suggestions.

and highlights the importance of the development of the domestic bond markets to promote long-lasting economic growth.

1.1. INTRODUCTION

The goal of every nation's economic policy is to ensure a high and stable level of economic growth. The importance of the development of a financial system that promotes economic growth and results in poverty reduction has been demonstrated by a number of empirical studies[2]. It is also well known that a country's public borrowing and its nature are important determinants of its economic performance. A most proposed channel for the public debt-growth connection relates to the extent to which heavy public debt burdens or debt service are likely to have significant negative implications on capital accumulation and reduce ("crowd out") investment necessary for productivity growth which, in all probability, results in the slowdown of economic growth. However, although a growing body of recent literature tries to uncover the relationship between public debt and economic growth, there is no compelling answers to the questions: How does debt accumulation interact with growth? To what extent and under what conditions can public debt be an impediment to growth? What is the growth impact of domestic versus external financing? Our empirical work aims to address these issues by providing new evidence regarding the debt-growth nexus across different subsets of countries. Yet, such analysis becomes even more relevant in light of the recent financial and economic crisis that has put explicit strains on public debt. There have begun to be serious concerns over the broader economic consequences of public debt buildups.

This paper contributes to previous empirical work in several important respects. First, it not only examines the growth effects of total public debt, but also distinguishes between the growth impact of domestic versus external public debt, focusing on the relevance of domestic public financing as compared to external public financing. In particular, we present a direct test of domestic versus external debt by controlling the institutional environment in which the debt was issued using appropriately specified growth equations. Second, it is sufficiently comprehensive in terms of country coverage to enable robust conclusions. Furthermore, we employ samples that are more likely to be

[2] King and Levine (1993), Rajan and Zingales (1998), Levine (1999, 2003, 2005), DemirgüÇ-Kunt, A. and R. Levine (2001), Greenwood and Jovanovic (1990), etc.

homogenous by splitting the countries into high-income, middle-income and low-income groups[3]. This econometric study covers the period between 1990-2007 and distinguishes countries by their income levels. Third, to assess whether the debt-growth relationship is influenced by country characteristics, we consider countries with differing policies and institutions and control for various measures of macroeconomic fundamentals, and financial and institutional factors. The set of variables encompasses the real per capita GDP growth, the level of financial development, law and order, ICRG composite risk rating, population growth, the savings rate, openness to trade, and inflation. Given the existence of different approaches which emphasize the substitute or complementary role of banks and markets on growth, we decided to control simultaneously the potential impact of banks and markets on growth to capture various channels of financial deepening. Namely, we chose liquid liabilities M2 to GDP (LLY) as a conventional variable to measure banking sector development and stock market capitalization (MCAP) to capture capital market development. Finally, our analysis exploited both static (FE estimator) and dynamic (GMM estimator) panel data techniques, which have a number of econometric advantages to grasp various aspects of indebtedness, financial development and institutional stability.

The remainder of the chapter is organized as follows. The next section discusses the related literature on public debt and growth, and the role of domestic versus external financing. The third section describes the data sources of the statistics. The fourth and fifth sections discuss the empirical methodology we adopt and report econometric estimates for the debt-growth nexus, distinguishing among different subsamples and differing country characteristics. The paper concludes with the sixth section.

1.2. Related Literature

Debt and growth have been connected in the literature in two different ways. On the good side, government debt can play an important role for growth, for instance, by raising funds for long-term development projects in physical infrastructure and human capital. Compared to other forms of budgetary finance, market based domestic borrowing is seen to contribute more to: macroeconomic stability (low inflation and reduced vulnerability to

[3] The split among high-income, middle-income and low-income countries is made along the WB classification.

external real and domestic monetary shocks), domestic savings and, private investment. Indeed, public debt can support a financial system in credit intermediation, or can act as a substitute for it and, at times, it can even help the financial system to survive crises.

In contrast, excessive public debt can have long-term negative consequences. Public debt can act as an implicit tax on the resources generated by a country (Barro 1979, 1995, Dotsey 1994) and create a burden on future generations which come in the form of a reduced flow of income from a lower stock of private capital (Modigliani 1961). This, in turn, may lead to an increase in long-term interest rates, a crowding out of private investments necessary for productivity growth, and a reduction in capital accumulation (Gale and Orzag 2003; Baldacci and Kumar 2010). A heavy public debt burden can also have significant negative implications for fiscal sustainability and, ultimately, severely stunt economic development and welfare. However, as external and domestic debt respond quite differently to the macroeconomic and political environment, there is increasing recognition that the development of domestic security markets and the related choice of the denomination of the debt instruments have important implications for the frequency of currency and financial crises (Allen, Borensztein, Yeyati, Panizza 2007; Hemming et al., 2003; Burnside et al., 2001). An analysis across the economic history of many countries, advanced and emerging, suggests a strong connection between debt cycles and economic crises (Reinhart and Rogoff 2010, a,b).

The empirical studies on the relationship between debt and growth primarily focused on the role of external debt in developing countries. Patillo et al., (2002) show how the debt-growth relationship evolves with indebtedness levels for developing countries over the period from 1960 to 1998 and assess the nonlinear relationship (in the form of an inverted U-shape) between total external debt and per capita GDP growth. In particular, they found, that the average impact of debt on growth becomes negative for net present value of debt levels above 35-40 percent of GDP. Furthermore, the analysis by Cordella et al., (2005) regarding HIPC[4] versus non-HIPC countries indicates that the relationship between external debt and growth depends on the level of debt and the quality of institutions and policies. Countries with good policies and institutions face overhang[5] (the indebtedness level above which the marginal effect of debt on growth becomes negative) when the debt

[4] Highly Indebted Poor Countries.

[5] The term "debt overhang" was introduced in the literature by Krugman (1988), as a situation in which a country's expected repayment ability on external debt falls below the contractual value of debt.

rises above 15-30 percent of GDP, but the marginal effect of debt on growth becomes irrelevant (the indebtedness level above which the marginal effect of debt on growth becomes zero) above 70-80 percent, while in countries with bad policies and institutions, overhang and irrelevance thresholds seem to be lower, and the possibility, that debt does not matter at all, cannot be ruled out. The relevance of countries' policies and institutions in terms of growth impact of public debt in low and middle-income countries was also emphasized by Imbs and Ranciere (2005), Harrabi et al., (2007), and Presbitero (2010). In addition, the results from Presbitero (2008) emphasizes that the external debt overhang seems to be at work exclusively in countries with sound institutions, while external debt proves to be irrelevant for countries with weak institutions. Other previous empirical studies on the nonlinear effects of debt on growth include Cohen (1997) for African and Latin American countries, Elbadawi (1997) for Sub-Saharan Africa, and Checherita et al., (2010) for the 12 euro area countries. It is worth noting that the specific magnitude of the effect of high debt on growth varies substantially across specifications.

On the other hand, Schclarek (2004) finds a linear negative impact of external debt on per capita GDP growth in a panel of developing countries and no evidence of a statistically significant relationship for a sample of industrial countries over the period of 1970 to 2002. In contrast, Kumar and Woo (2010) highlight linear negative effects of initial debt levels for subsequent growth in advanced and emerging economies after controlling for other determinants of growth over the period from 1970 to 2007. Yet, a study by Reinhart and Rogoff (2010, a), who analyzed the development of public debt and the long-term real GDP growth rate in a sample of 20 developed countries over a period spanning about two centuries (1790-2009), shows (through simple correlation statistics) that median growth rates fall by one percent, and average growth falls considerably more for debt/GDP ratios above a debt threshold of 90 percent of GDP. Distinguishing between advanced and emerging economies, they find that the threshold for total public debt is similar, while for external debt (public and private), which is usually denominated in a foreign currency, emerging markets face lower thresholds. In particular, when external debt reaches 60 percent of GDP, annual growth declines by about one percent; for higher levels, growth rates are roughly cut in half. Moreover, focusing on the economic consequences of high burdens of external debt in poor countries, Presbitero (2006) also found a linear and negative relationship between external debt and growth. The magnitude of the debt effect on GDP growth estimated in this study is much larger in the LICs and HIPCs, than in the rest of the sample, suggesting that heavy indebtedness is a critical issue in the world's poorest countries.

As noted by Jeanne and Guscina (2006), while the total public debt to GDP ratio does not vary much across developed and developing economies, there are marked differences across countries regarding their reliance on domestic debt. Alli Abbas and Christiansen (2007) explored the impact of domestic debt in low-income and emerging market countries. They found that moderate levels of domestic debt, as a share of GDP and bank deposits, had a positive overall impact on growth through a variety of channels (improved monetary policy, broader financial market development, enhanced private saving and financial intermediation), while above a threshold level of 35% of bank deposits, domestic debt began to undermine growth.

We take into account that domestic debt is a significant and growing portion of countries' total level of indebtedness and not only examine the growth effect of total public debt, but also distinguish between domestic versus external components of public financing and test the growth impact of domestic versus external debt by controlling the institutional environment in which the debt was issued. This framework avoids the problem that domestic debt could proxy for eventually omitted variables and, especially, for financial development.

1.3. THE DATA AND STYLIZED FACTS

This econometric study covers the period from 1990 to 2007 and distinguishes countries by their income levels. In particular, in this study we employ samples that are more likely to be homogenous by splitting the countries into high-income, middle income and low-income groups[6]. High income group includes: "High income: OECD" and "High income: non OECD" countries; Middle income group includes: "Upper middle income" and "Lower middle income" countries while Low income group includes: "Low income" countries as classified in the WB database.

The data are from various sources. We constructed our dependent variable GDP per capita growth by employing GDP per capita (constant 2000 US$) from the WDI database published by the World Bank. Given that the debt that

[6] The list of countries are reported on Appendix I. The split among high-income, middle-income and low-income countries is made along the WB classification.

has a policy relevance is the public debt[7], our research looks at public debt and economic growth connections. To capture the composition of public debt, we employ a new dataset introduced by Panizza (2008) covering up to 130 countries for the period of 1990-2007. The important feature of this dataset is that it presents the possibility to disaggregate the total public debt data into its domestic and external components. Public debt classification includes: central government debt, general government and non-financial public sector debt. To evaluate the impact of debt on growth, we alternately employed the ratios of Total Debt-to-GDP, External Debt-to-GDP, and Domestic Debt-to-GDP. Data on GDP values in U.S. dollars also are from the dataset introduced by Panizza (2008).

The indicators of financial development (LLY and MCAP) are taken from the "New Database on Financial Development and Structure (2010)" by Thorsten Beck, Asli Demirguc-Kunt and Ross Eric Levine. To assess whether the debt-growth relationship is influenced by country characteristics, we employed "The Composite Political, Financial, and Economic risk Rating index"[8] and "Law and Order"[9] from the International Country Risk Guide (ICRG). Other macroeconomic variables such as inflation (measured as annual growth rates of the consumer price index), Savings rate, Trade openness[10] and Population growth come from the World Development Indicators Database. Definitions and data sources for all variables used in the empirical analysis are reported on Table 1. Descriptive statistics are provided on Table 2: "Panel a" presents "Summary statistics" and "Panel b" presents the "Correlation matrix" by subsamples. The mean total public debt-to-GDP ratio is 0.60 for the middle-income sample, 0.47 for the high-income sample and 1.1 for the low-income sample. In effect, about 37 percent of observations fall above the 60 percent Maastricht criteria for the middle-income sample, while 27 percent of observations for the high income sample and 68 percent of observations for the low-income sample are above the Maastricht criteria.

---

7 The public debt shows the degree to which the government must rely on private savings (or the "debt market") to finance borrowing. The competition for these private resources could lead to higher interest rates and so-called crowding out of private investments. The private sector debt does not have the same impact.

8 This index ranges from 1 to 6. The index rises as the risk reduces and stability increases. It can be used as a proxy for institutional quality as good institutions affect risk and stability.

9 Law and Order are assessed separately, with each sub-component comprising zero to three points. The Law sub-component is an assessment of the strength and impartiality of the legal system, while the Order sub-component is an assessment of popular observance of the law.

10 Index suggested by Rajan and Zingales (2003), i.e. the sum of exports and imports of goods and services as a share of GDP.

Table 1. The Data Description and Sources

Variable	Description	Sources
Domestic debt/total debt	Domestic Public debt-to-Total debt ratio	Dataset introduced by Panizza (2008)
Total debt/GDP	Total Public debt-to-GDP ratio	Dataset introduced by Panizza (2008)
External debt/GDP	External Public Debt-to-GDP ratio	Dataset introduced by Panizza (2008)
Domestic debt/GDP	Domestic Public Debt-to-GDP ratio	Dataset introduced by Panizza (2008)
Per capita real GDP	GDP per capita in constant 2000 US$	World Development Indicators
GDP per capita growth	Annual per capita GDP growth constructed as log difference of per capita real GDP	World Development Indicators
GDP	GDP in current US$	Dataset introduced by Panizza (2008)
Law and order	Law and Order are assessed separately, with each sub-component comprising zero to three points. The Law sub-component is an assessment of the strength and impartiality of the legal system, while the Order sub-component is an assessment of popular observance of the law.	ICRG Database
Quality of Bureaucracy	High points are given to countries where the bureaucracy has the strength and expertise to govern without drastic changes in policy or interruptions in government services. In the low-risk countries, the bureaucracy tends to be somewhat autonomous from political pressure and to have an established mechanism for recruitment and training. Countries that lack the cushioning effect of a strong bureaucracy receive low points because a change in government tends to be traumatic in terms of policy formulation and day-to-day administrative functions.	ICRG Database
Government stability	A measure of government's ability to carry out its declared programs, and its ability to stay in office.	ICRG Database

Variable	Description	Sources
	This will depend on the type of governance, the cohesion of the government and governing party or parties, the closeness of the next election, the government's command of the legislature, popular approval of government policies, and so on.	
ICRG Risk index	Composite Political, Financial, and Economic risk Rating. The index rises as the risk reduces and stability increases. It can be used as a proxy for institutional quality as good institutions affect risk and stability.	ICRG Database
Inflation	Annual change in CPI index in logs.	World Development Indicators
Exchange rate volatility	Real Exchange rate volatility (std. deviation) over the last 5 years.	World Development Indicators
Trade Openness	Trade to GDP ratio measured as the sum of exports and imports of goods and services as a share of GDP.	World Development Indicators
Savings	Gross Domestic Savings (% of GDP).	World Development Indicators
Population Growth	Annual Population Growth	World Development Indicators
LLY	Ratio of liquid liabilities of the financial system to GDP (currency plus demand and interest-bearing liabilities of bank and nonbank financial intermediaries).	WB database[11]
PRIVO	Ratio to GDP of credit issued to the private sector by banks and other financial intermediaries.	WB database
BTOT	Ratio of commercial bank assets to the sum of commercial bank assets and central bank assets.	WB database
MCAP	Stock market capitalization relative to GDP.	WB database
TOR	Ratio of trades in domestic shares to market capitalization (Turnover Ratio).	WB database
OVC	Ratio of overhead costs to total bank assets.	WB database

[11] WB New database on financial development and structure, introduced by Thorsten Beck, Asli Demirguc-Kunt and Ross Eric Levine.

Table 1. (Continued)

Variable	Description	Sources
NIM	Difference between bank interest income and interest expenses, divided by total assets (Net Interest Margin).	WB database
TVT	Ratio of trades in domestic shares (on domestic exchanges) to GDP, as indicators of stock market activity (Total value traded).	WB database
FD	Overall financial development, constructed from LLY, PRIVO, BTOT, OVC, NIM, MCAP, TVT TOR.	See text
FDSIZE	Size of financial system, constructed from LLY and MCAP	See text
FDEFF	Financial efficiency, constructed from OVC, NIM, TVT and TOR	See text
FDBANK	Extent of bank based intermediation, constructed from LLY, PRIVO, BTOT, OVC and NIM	See text
FDSTOCK	Stock market development measure, constructed from MCAP, TVT and TOR	See text
FDEPTH	Financial depth, constructed from LLY, PRIVO and BTOT	See text

Figure 1.a shows scatter plots of total public debt against per capita GDP growth, whereas Figure 1.b presents external and domestic public debt shares against per capita GDP growth to see whether or not there appears to be a clear trend between debt levels and growth in countries grouped by income levels. As one can see from the scatter plots, there are marked differences regarding the association between debt and per capita GDP growth across different country subsamples. Clearly, scatterplots do not reveal a systematic pattern as well as any non - linearities in public debt - growth connection showing that high debt levels lead to lower growth in different groups of countries. We explore this relationship using econometric analysis.

1.4. METHODOLOGY

We investigated the growth impact of public debt by controlling the institutional environment in which the debt was issued.

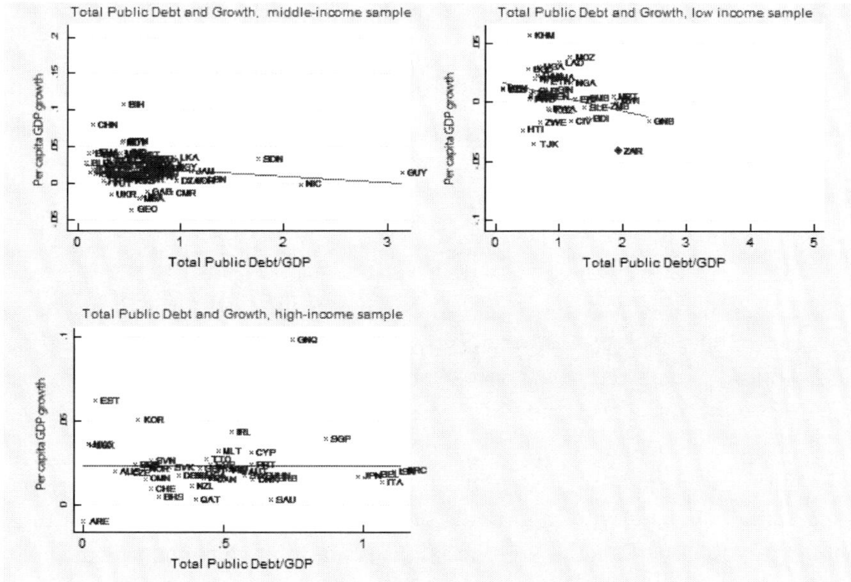

Figure 1a. Total Public Debt and per capita GDP growth, by income group.

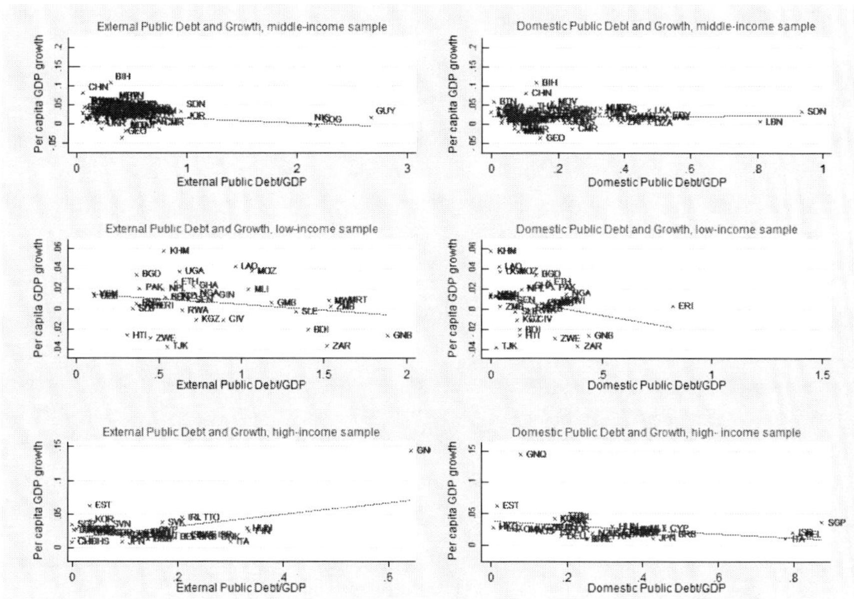

Figure 1b. External/Domestic Public Debt and per capita GDP Growth, by income groups.

Following most of the literature on debt and growth, we specified a quadratic[12] relationship between Total Public Debt and Per Capita GDP Growth to investigate the non-linear effects of public debt accumulation on growth via the following basic AR (1) panel data model:

$$Y_{it} = \varphi_1 Y_{it-1} + \varphi_2 ToTDebt_{it-1} + \varphi_3 ToTDebt_{it-1}^2 + \varphi_4 H_i ToTDebt_{it-1} + \\ + \varphi_5 H_i ToTDebt_{it-1}^2 + \varphi_6 FD_{it-1} + \varphi_7 X_{it-1} + \eta_i + \xi_{it} \quad (1)$$

where, Y_{it} denotes country i's (i = 1,..., N) per capita GDP growth in year t. We assumed that the current period growth variables are mainly affected by previous period explanatory variables and, as is standard in this literature, we lagged all our control variables by one period. Thus, $ToTDebt_{it-1}$ is the (one period) lagged values of the Total Public Debt-to-GDP Ratio[13]; $ToTDebt_{it-1}^2$ is a quadratic Total debt-to-GDP term in year (t-1); H_i is a dummy variable representing countries with high total debt[14] to test whether the effect of total debt on growth is the same in high-debt versus non-high debt countries; X_{it-1} is a group of controls, including the (one period) lagged values of the log of initial GDP per capita, trade openness, gross domestic savings (% of GDP), domestic/external public debt shares in total public debt, composite political, financial, and economic risk rating, population growth, and log of CPI-based current inflation to smooth out hyperinflation spikes; FD_{it-1} is an indicator of financial development in year (t-1). The model allows for unobserved heterogeneity through the latent variable η_i capturing time invariant country components and ε_{it} represents the usual disturbance terms.

To capture the effects of domestic versus external public financing on growth we split up the total public debt variable into its domestic and external subcomponents and estimated the following equations, specifically testing for domestic versus external indebtedness levels:

$$Y_{it} = \varphi_1 Y_{it-1} + \varphi_2 ExDebt_{it-1} + \varphi_3 ExDebt_{it-1}^2 + \varphi_4 H_i ExDebt_{it-1} + \\ + \varphi_5 H_i ExDebt_{it-1}^2 + \varphi_9 FD_{it-1} + \varphi_{10} X_{it-1} + \eta_i + \xi_{it}$$

---

[12] Quadratic model allows the marginal effect of debt on growth to change according to the extent of indebtedness.

[13] By using lagged levels of debt to examine the impact on subsequent growth of real per capita GDP we also try to avoid the reverse causality problem as slower growth rates can lead to high debt buildups rather than high debt is lowering growth.

[14] Considering the existing evidence, the split between the highly indebted versus non-highly indebted countries was made to find the model that best fits the data. In particular, we identified as highly indebted, countries with a total debt-to-GDP ratio above 90 percent in high and middle-income countries' subsets, while our findings support a 100 percent ratio of total debt-to-GDP in the low-income group.

and

$$Y_{it} = \varphi_1 Y_{it-1} + \varphi_6 DomDebt_{it-1} + \varphi_7 DomDebt_{it-1}^2 + \\ + \varphi_8 (DomDebt*High\_FD)_{it-1} + \varphi_9 FD_{it-1} + \varphi_{10} X_{it-1} + \eta_i + \xi_{it} \qquad (2)$$

where, $ExDebt_{it-1}$ denotes country i's external public debt relative to GDP in year (t-1); H_i is a dummy variable representing countries with high external debt[15] to test whether the effect of external debt on growth is the same in high-debt versus non-high debt countries; $DomDebt_{it-1}$ denotes country i's domestic public debt relative to GDP in year (t-1); $(DomDebt*High\_FD)_{it-1}$ is an interaction term between the domestic debt share and financial development variables. In order to test whether the effect of domestic debt on growth is the same in countries with high level of financial development[16] versus less-financially developed, we interact the High_FD dummy with the domestic debt variable. If φ_8 coefficients were found to be positive and statistically significant, then this would imply that the combination of financial development and development of domestic debt markets exerts an independent influence on growth, over any influence each of these two variables may separately have on growth. Again, X_{it-1} is a group of standard controls, FD_{it-1} is an indicator of financial development, η_i captures time invariant country components and ξ_{it} represents the usual disturbance terms.

By following the large number of empirical growth studies, we identified the priors on the coefficients of our control variables. Namely, initial per capita GDP, in accordance with Solow's convergence hypothesis, should have a negative impact on growth. A high burden of total public debt and a high share of external public debt were expected to impact growth non-linearly. The population growth rate was also expected to reduce real per capita growth. A low inflation is considered a pre-condition for lasting growth. The impacts of financial development, institutional quality and trade openness on growth may differ by income group and by stage of development.

In estimating our panel growth model, we started with a FE estimation[17]. While such estimates shed light on the main forces at work, we also present

---

[15] We identified as highly indebted, countries above a 90 percent ratio of external debt-to-GDP in high and middle-income countries' subsets, while our findings support a 100 percent ratio of external debt-to-GDP in the low-income group.

[16] High_FD countries are defined as countries above the median level of financial development by subsamples.

[17] In the context of our growth regression , we dropped a lagged dependent variable as a regressor to get consistent estimates with FE estimator.

regressions based on the GMM estimator[18] in accordance with the recent empirical growth literature. Specifically, we applied the two-step version of the expanded GMM estimator with "Windmeijer finite-sample correction" to the standard errors. This dynamic panel data technique allows us to control for unobservable country-specific factors as well as for potential endogeneity of some explanatory variables. The indicators of financial development were treated as potentially endogenous and instrumented by their own lagged values and the lagged values of the external instrument "low and order"[19]. To keep a sensible relationship between the number of cross-sectional observations and the number of over-identifying restrictions, generally only less distant lags (second to third lags) were used as instruments for non-strictly exogenous variables included in the regression. The GMM framework implies the lack of autocorrelation in idiosyncratic error term ξ_{it}. We used the standard Arellano-Bond (1991) tests for serial correlation in the first-differenced errors. The first-order serial correlation was expected in the differenced errors, but model identification requires absence of second-order serial correlation.

The Windmeijer (2005) finite sample correction to the standard errors was adopted for two-step GMM estimators, and Sargan-Hansen's test was used to assess the model specification and over identifying restrictions. We calculated a point estimate for the long-run effect[20] of different indebtedness measures as well as for some control variables on growth: $\beta_{LR}=\beta/(1-\varphi)$, where β is the coefficient of interest on a measure of debt variable or some controls estimated in the regression and φ is the coefficient on the lagged dependent variable, to examine whether increases in indebtedness level or changes in chosen control variables affect growth, and whether this effect persists in the long-run. An approximate standard error for this long-run effect was estimated using the delta method.

In order to test on the presence of an inverted U-shaped relationship between debt and growth, we also employed the delta method. Tables 1 through 5, in Appendix II, present the results of the Country Fixed Effects (FE) and GMM Estimation of our regressions. The results described in what follows were consistent across specifications and estimation strategies. The pattern emerged is along the lines of the stated priors.

---

[18] available in STATA with *xtabond2* option (Roodman (2006)).

[19] Following La Pota et al., (1998). They showed that a country's legal origins are the central driving factor for financial development. Since most countries obtained their legal systems through occupation and colonization, this variable may be plausibly treated as exogenous.

[20] Available in STATA with "nlcom" option, which takes nonlinear combination of the estimated coefficients and computes standard errors using the delta method.

1.5. Estimation Results

This section presents the results of our panel data analysis. We first estimated equation (1) for different country subsamples and test for countries' total indebtedness levels alongside measures of financial development, macroeconomic fundamentals and institutional factors. Table 1 (Appendix II) reports the results of the Country Fixed Effect estimator by subsamples with and without including separate debt shares. We mostly focus our discussion on the regressions estimated by the GMM (2-step) estimator, which also controls for potential endogeneity of all explanatory variables[21], reported in table 2 (Appendix II)[22], by country groups respectively. Recall that, in the case of GMM estimator, we report Arellano-Bond tests for second order serial correlation in errors as well as the Hansen statistics. This diagnostic tests support the model's specification, in particular, the Hansen statistics do not reject the over-identifying restrictions, confirming the validity of the instruments and the Arellano-Bond tests for serial correlation do not reject the hypothesis of no autocorrelation of the second order. We also report point estimates and approximate standard errors of the debt turning points and the long-run effects of chosen explanatory variables.

1.5.1. The Impact of Total Public Debt on Growth

The regressions' outcome points clearly in the direction of a non-linear (an inverted U-shape) relationship between total public debt-to-GDP and per capita GDP growth variables in the non-highly indebted middle and low-income counties' subsets only. In fact, the coefficient on total public debt-to-GDP variable is positively signed and significant and that of squared total public debt-to-GDP is negatively signed and significant in most estimations for these subsets. Hence, our samples capture the evidence of the total public debt overhang found in the literature with respect to gross external debt (Pattillo et al., 2002, Cordela et al., 2005[23], among others).

---

[21] GMM estimator controls for endogeneity by using "internal instruments", i.e. instruments based on lagged values of the explanatory variables.

[22] For high-income countries the results of the GMM regressions by including separate debt shares alongside total debt variable, are not presented due to space considerations. However, our findings for this variable sets suggest no significant relationship between them and growth.

[23] Cordella et al., (2005) and Pattillo et al., (2002) examined the effects of total external debt (public and private) for HIPCs and non-HIPCs samples.

Table 2. Descriptive Statistics, 1990-2007

**a. Summary Statistics by subsamples:
Middle-income sample**

Variable	Observation	Mean	Std. Dev.	Min	Max
Per capita GDP growth	1598	0.0221886	0.0649417	-0.5810032	0.6443257
Totaldebt/GDP	1163	0.6002244	0.5853149	0.0043804	6.934951
Totaldebt/gdp>0.6	434	1.041117	0.7555799	0.6005736	6.934951
External debt/GDP	1145	0.4485174	0.5562236	0	6.934951
Domestic debt/GDP	1105	0.2023177	0.2111274	0	1.269725
LLY	1327	0.4552279	0.2764361	0.0019442	1.489408
MCAP	814	0.3331289	0.4373926	0.0002124	3.084334
PRIVO	1321	0.3353278	0.2629232	0.0011415	1.659618
Initial per capita GDP	1690	7.488024	0.7814207	5.563274	9.201808
Inflation	1491	2.061788	1.471001	-3.244194	8.920214
Population growth	1474	0.0132609	0.0269483	-0.298541	0.4749091
Saving rate	1542	1.652231	1.702538	-7.182182	7.149847
Trade	1575	8.825293	4.092009	1.108743	28.34363
ICR index	1143	6.510634	0.9900032	2.3	8.48

High-income sample

Variable	Observation	Mean	Std. Dev.	Min	Max
Per capita GDP growth	868	0.0240933	0.0426024	-0.1575174	0.5054407
Totaldebt/GDP	726	0.4796794	0.3349306	0	2.073809
Totaldebtgdp>0.6	195	0.9191042	0.266739	0.6010929	2.073809
External debt/GDP	522	0.1543209	0.1978995	0	1.896468
Domestic debt/GDP	528	0.3184258	0.2351391	0	1.283778
LLY	778	0.8317609	0.5381082	0.0473482	4.317595
MCAP	717	0.7535722	0.6893171	0.0143547	6.034795
PRIVO	797	0.8616822	0.4478151	0.0236798	2.697557
Initial per capita GDP	921	9.690537	0.685124	6.258056	11.19324
Inflation	877	1.16505	1.181517	-4.017384	10.07631
Population growth	881	0.0145772	0.0406704	-0.3615023	0.700129
Saving rate	826	2.76194	1.276467	-6.695316	8.688134
Trade	849	10.48855	6.660469	1.610839	45.66461
ICR index	822	8.019816	0.6868401	2.55	9.35

Table 2. (Continued)
Low-income sample

Variable	Observation	Mean	Std. Dev.	Min	Max
Per capita GDP growth	783	0.0076207	0.0706248	-0.6328516	0.6425905
Totaldebt/GDP	482	1.100644	1.508475	0.0038443	20.22333
Totaldebtgdp>0.6	327	1.431353	1.73276	0 .6007468	20.22333
External debt/GDP	495	0.8090101	0.6066712	0.0038443	4.04572
Domestic debt/GDP	470	0.2844621	1.192216	0	17.98992
LLY	660	0.255062	0.1295708	0.0315688	1.101823
MCAP	200	0.1620137	0.2606723	0.0007758	2.89289
PRIVO	663	0.1373934	0.0985068	0.003967	0.9055625
Initial per capita GDP	827	5.669204	0.5310073	4.130945	7.231881
Inflation	779	2.312221	1.23766	-2.918771	9.254602
Population growth	798	0.0259285	0.031299	-0.3323696	0.5232455
Saving rate	773	0.679138	1.226244	-4.850794	4.607472
Trade	817	6.342954	2.923052	0.0308803	19.96796
ICR index	601	5.500466	1.076651	1.4	7.28

b. Correlation matrix
Middle-income sample

	PPP growth	Tot.debt	Ex.debt	Dom.debt	LLY	MCAP	In.GDP	Infl.	Populat.	Saving	Trade	ICRG
PPP growth	1.0000											
Tot.debt	-0.1114	1.0000										
Ex.dept	-0.1290	0.9390	1.0000									
Dom.debt	-0.0675	0.5039	0.1936	1.0000								
LLY	-0.0322	0.0845	-0.0264	0.2314	1.0000							
MCAP	0.0347	0.0408	-0.1023	0.2580	0.5151	1.0000						
In. GDP	0.0664	-0.2649	-0.2874	-0.0400	0.2661	0.2008	1.0000					
Inflation	-0.2837	0.1475	0.1089	0.0225	-0.3921	-0.1558	-0.1966	1.0000				
Population	-0.0251	0.0118	0.0514	0.0020	-0.0130	0.0885	-0.0135	-0.0137	1.0000			
Saving rate	0.0592	-0.1768	-0.0853	-0.1089	-0.0029	0.1086	0.2235	-0.0207	0.0757	1.0000		
Trade	0.0218	0.1206	0.2274	-0.1059	0.4164	0.2012	0.0176	-0.1513	0.0145	-0.0344	1.000	
ICRG	0.2625	-0.4343	-0.4012	-0.2735	0.2929	0.2724	0.4827	-0.4403	-0.0945	0.3152	0.140	1.00

Table 2. (Continued)

High-income sample

	PPP growth	Tot.debt	Ex.debt	Dom.debt	LLY	MCAP	In.GDP	Infl.	Populat.	Saving	Trade	ICRG
PPP growth	1.0000											
Tot.debt	-0.0830	1.0000										
Ex.debt	0.0312	0.6475	1.0000									
Dom. debt	-0.1454	0.7725	0.0188	1.0000								
LLY	-0.1160	-0.0251	-0.3296	0.1357	1.0000							
MCAP	0.0641	-0.1089	-0.3065	0.0703	0.5512	1.0000						
In.GDP	-0.1908	-0.1178	-0.5141	0.2490	0.4469	0.5021	1.0000					
Inflation	-0.0018	0.0019	0.2359	-0.1106	-0.1936	-0.2348	-0.3809	1.0000				
Population	0.3374	-0.0266	0.1813	-0.0533	-0.1009	0.0591	-0.1469	0.0419	1.0000			
Saving	0.3022	-0.3255	-0.3168	-0.1046	0.1832	0.2783	0.1129	-0.0972	0.3928	1.0000		
Trade	0.2173	-0.1522	-0.0533	0.0404	0.3923	0.4864	-0.0310	0.0447	0.0900	0.3525	1.000	
ICRG	0.1274	-0.1450	-0.3242	0.0028	0.3494	0.3386	0.5658	-0.4040	0.0078	0.3326	0.124	1.00

Low-income sample

	PPP growth	Tot.debt	Ex.debt	Dom.debt	LLY	MCAP	In.GDP	Infl.	Populat.	Saving	Trade	ICRG
PPP growth	1.0000											
Tot.debt	-0.2184	1.0000										
Ex.debt	-0.1497	0.6767	1.0000									
Dom.debt	-0.2408	0.9213	0.3395	1.0000								
LLY	-0.0031	-0.0806	-0.1918	0.3464	1.0000							
MCAP	-0.3295	-0.0324	-0.2130	0.4273	0.1669	1.0000						
In.GDP	0.1060	-0.3887	-0.4227	-0.1431	0.3142	0.3350	1.0000					
Inflation	-0.2075	0.1303	0.0981	0.1082	-0.0676	0.4202	-0.0385	1.0000				
Population	0.1541	0.0294	0.0670	-0.0118	-0.0726	-0.2462	-0.0308	- 0.0488	1.0000			
Saving	0.1259	-0.3226	-0.2649	-0.2466	0.2863	0.1013	0.3982	-0.0263	0.0145	1.0000		
Trade	0.1041	0.1029	0.0969	0.0746	0.1377	0.2534	0.2747	0.0272	-0.0071	0.0745	1.000	
ICRG index	0.3549	-0.2714	-0.2352	-0.0955	0.2730	-0.2408	0.4234	-0.3828	0.0122	0.4025	0.3739	1.0

That is, on average for observed middle and low-income countries public debt-to-GDP ratios would have a negative impact on growth after a certain threshold has been reached. However, no significant relationship is found for middle income countries with a debt above 90 percent of GDP and low-income countries with debt above 100 percent of GDP, implying that economic growth is not sensitive to further debt accumulation (debt irrelevance) in this countries. Heavy debt burdens are likely to worsen macroeconomic policies and increase policy volatility. This, in turn, may lead to an irrelevant effect of debt on economic growth.

We estimated a turning point of a debt overhang (i.e. a threshold at which the marginal effect of total public debt on growth turns negative) using a delta method. The suggested threshold value of a total public debt-to-GDP ratio lies around 0.8 for middle-income countries and is strongly statistically significant, while the threshold is lower and lies around 0.7 for low income countries and is also statistically significant (see table 2, Appendix II). Considering the results of previous studies, our growth maximizing debt thresholds are slightly higher implying that in our sample, debt overhang and/or irrelevance is at work only for higher levels of public debt. The general explanation for the different threshold values is likely to be different sources employed for a "debt variable" and different debt data completeness. Our key differences with respect to previous works is to look at government borrowing (not gross debt) and economic growth connections, given that the debt that is economically relevant is the public debt. We employ a new dataset introduced by Panizza (2008), where public debt classification refers mainly to central government debt, and do not take into account a component of private sector debt. Other studies [i.e. Patillo et al., (2002, 2004), Cordella et al., (2005), Kumar and Woo (2010) etc.], however, mainly employ gross external debts from the GDF dataset published by World Bank or the IMF WEO dataset. Yet, the "total external debt stocks"[1] variable as well as "external debt stocks, public and publicly guaranteed"[2] variable from GDF includes public and private (publicly

[1] External debt stocks, total (DOD, current US$) -Total external debt is debt owed to nonresidents repayable in foreign currency, goods, or services. Total external debt is the sum of public, publicly guaranteed, and private nonguaranteed long-term debt, use of IMF credit, and short-term debt. Short-term debt includes all debt having an original maturity of one year or less and interest in arrears on long-term debt. Data are in current U.S. dollars. Source: World Bank, Global Development Finance.

[2] External debt stocks, public and publicly guaranteed (PPG) (DOD, current US$) - Public and publicly guaranteed debt comprises long-term external obligations of public debtors, including the national government, political subdivisions (or an agency of either), and autonomous public bodies, and external obligations of private debtors that are guaranteed

guaranteed) components of external debt. Moreover, GDF does not cover advanced economies. The WEO dataset also refers to general gross government and consists of general government debt as well as part of the public guarantees under a standard scheme. Further, a study by Reinhart and Rogoff (2010) looks at levels of gross debt, and, thus, it additionally tracks holdings under explicit government guarantees. They also employed interpolations and other data transformations to build continuous data series. For assessing the economic impact of public debt, economists generally agree that public debt, as opposed to gross debt, is the more correct measure because it shows the degree to which the government must rely on private savings (or the "debt market") to finance borrowing. It is the competition for these private resources that could lead to higher interest rates and so-called crowding out of private investments. Debt issued by the private sector does not have the same impact. Consequently, since the main debt variable we employ consists of only a public debt component and does not account for a private component of debt our findings differ and so do the debt thresholds identified by our analysis.

Additionally, in comparing our study to previous empirical works, other differences include: a) sample populations by different country groupings (we study countries grouped by income levels, while Patillo et al., (2002, 2004) and Cordella et al., (2005) study HIPCs versus non-HIPCs. A study by Reinhard and Rogoff distinguishes advanced versus emerging economies); b) different dimensions of time explored and, finally, c) differences in methodological approach. More specifically on the last point, the study by Reinhard and Rogoff (2010) examines only yearly GDP growth and debt levels through simple correlation statistics with no allowance for a dynamic relation. Their findings do not take into account other determinants of growth or issues such as reverse causality (as slower growth rates can lead to high debt buildups rather than high debt lowering growth)[3]. Obviously, debt thresholds are importantly country-specific[4] as country–specific factors affect the way in which debt affect the economy. Therefore, country groupings studied here merit further sensitivity analysis in light of the more comprehensive cross-country data on public debt.

for repayment by a public entity. Data are in current U.S. dollars. Source: World Bank, Global Development Finance.

[3] Irons and Bivens (2010).

[4] However, the consequences of higher debt levels for growth will be different country by country. As due to the fact that, in our sample of countries, number of observations for cross-country regressions are relatively small and, therefore, are subject to considerable uncertainly, the results by country are not reported.

Furthermore, the ratio of external public debt in total debt appears to have a negative impact on growth, which is statistically significant in the case of the GMM estimator for middle-income countries (table 2, column 2, Appendix II), pointing to a more detrimental impact of the higher external public debt shares in Total debt even below the threshold. In the middle-income sample we also found a stable negative long-run effect of high external debt shares in Total debt. For the rest of subsamples, a statistically significant negative coefficient on the external debt relative to Total debt was observed in high-income countries only with FE estimator (regression 8, table 1, Appendix II). In the next stage, this results prompted an investigation into the growth contribution of each component of public debt by splitting up the total public debt into external and domestic public debt components.

A particularly remarkable result is, that we do not find any support for a non-linear relationship between total public debt and growth for high-income countries. This results are suggestive of the interpretation, that high public debt levels for high-income countries are not necessarily associated with lower per capita GDP growth rates. The observed effect is consistent with those obtained by Schclarek (2004) for industrial countries.

As expected, in accordance with Solow's convergence hypothesis, the initial level of per capita GDP negatively correlates with growth (tables 1 and 2, Appendix II), while a statistically significant negative coefficients on initial level of GDP per capita were observed only in low-income sample. Coming to macroeconomic instability proxied by inflation, the coefficient estimates are negative across all samples and especially robust in the middle-income sample, suggesting that a 10 percentage point increase in the consumer price index tends to worsen the long-run growth by about a tenth of a percentage point. On the other hand, consistent with other results in the literature, trade to GDP ratio, used as a proxy for the level of openness of the economy, positively affects growth in middle and high-income countries (tables 1 and 2). Indeed, we also observe a robust long-run effect of trade openness in given subsets. In particular, a one standard deviation (4.09) increase in trade openness causes long-run increase of growth by 0.04 in middle-income sample, while a one standard deviation (6.9) increase in trade openness for high income countries causes long-run increase of growth by 0.14. The impact of openness on growth for low income countries is mainly negative (although not statistically significant) in specifications reported on tables 1 and 2.

However, simultaneously considering the potential roles of banks (LLY) and markets (MCAP) to proxy financial development in our analysis, in turn, permits to provide evidence to policy makers on the independent roles of markets and banks in the process of growth. Our results suggest that an increase in the level of financial development (proxied by MCAP) is associated with a surge in per capita GDP growth in the middle-income sample (tables 1 and 2). This effect is robust and there is fairly strong evidence that the effect persists in the long-run. Moreover, these results are consistent with the view that stock market liquidity facilitates long-run growth (Levine, 1991; Holmstrom and Tirole, 1993) and inconsistent with models that emphasize the negative aspects of stock market liquidity (Bhide, 1993). The estimates on LLY in the group of low-income countries are positive and, for most specifications, statistically significant (table 1 and 2). In the high-income subset a statistically significant positive correlation between financial development (proxied by MCAP) and growth is observed only with the FE estimator. Yet, in the group of high-income countries somewhat less precise estimates on indicators of financial development with the GMM estimator may reflect the fact that these countries by 1990 had already reached the stage of development of their financial sector, and observed financial indicators did not carry major weight for the time period of 1990 to 2007.

Our findings provide support for the hypothesis that the quality of institutions is a potentially important factor for long-term growth. In particular, a positive correlation is observed between the institutions variable (proxied by the composite risk index from ICRG) and growth for the most part of observations, while in the middle and high-income subsets the coefficients are strongly statistically significant when we only allow for country fixed effects estimates (table 1). It is also worth noting, that we find a positive and statistically significant effect of a high savings rate in the middle and high-income countries and the detrimental effect of population growth for the high-income countries in estimations reported on table 1.

1.5.2. The Impact of Domestic versus External Public Debt on Growth

In the next stage, the above estimation was complemented by the estimation framework of the equations (2), which allows an exploration of the growth contributions of external versus domestic components of public debt. On tables 3 through 5 (Appendix II) we report the results of different specifications, specifically testing for external versus domestic indebtedness levels along with measures of macroeconomic fundamentals and financial and institutional factors, applying the FE and GMM estimators for different country subsamples. The former table reports results for the high-income countries' group while the latter tables do the same for the middle-income and low-income countries' groups respectively. The results are quite robust across most of the specifications.

Our analysis supports the effect of external public debt overhang in the non - highly indebted middle and low-income counties' subsets. Hence, external public debt levels beyond a certain threshold dampen growth for the middle and low-income countries. We estimated a turning point of an external debt overhang (i.e. a threshold at which the marginal effect of external public debt on growth turns negative). Our results, reported in table 4, suggest that for the sample of middle-income countries the external public debt/GDP turning point is hovering around 0.7 (table 4), while the threshold is lower and lies around 0.6 for the low-income countries subsample (table 5). However, our growth maximizing debt to GDP ratio of 60 percent for the low-income countries is lower than that obtained by Elbadawi et al., (1997) for developing countries, which implies a growth maximizing debt to GDP ratio of 97 percent. Our threshold is higher than that estimated by Cordella et al., (2005), which shows an overhang ratio of 15 to 30 percent of debt-to-GDP, as well as by Pattilo et al., (2002), which supports a 35 to 40 percent debt-to-GDP ratio.

The differences in the results may be driven by reasons described above. Furthermore, our findings support an irrelevance threshold of 90 percent of GDP over which debt becomes irrelevant to growth for the middle-income countries, while the evidence of a clear cutoff for debt irrelevance is weaker in the low-income countries (because external debt-to-GDP as well as quadratic debt terms still have a marginally statistically significant impact on growth above a 100 percent debt-to-GDP ratio), but we cannot rule out the possibility that debt is irrelevant in this subset.

In our sample of middle-income countries, only about 14 percent of observations belong to the "debt irrelevance" (above the 90 percent external public debt-to-GDP cutoff) region for per capita GDP growth, while in a sample of low-income countries, this region (above the 100 percent external public debt-to-GDP cutoff) comprises almost 27 percent of the sample population.

The ratio of external public debt-to-total debt still prove to be linearly associated with growth having a negative and statistically precisely estimated impact for middle-income countries (table 4) and pointing, again, to a more detrimental impact of the higher external public debt shares in total debt even below the threshold.

In the case of GMM estimator, we also found a stable negative long-run effect, and one that is significantly different from zero at the 1 percent level in specifications reported on table 4. Yet, The coefficients on external debt share in total debt have unstable sign in the rest of subsamples.

Interestingly, we did not find evidence of any robust non-linear relationship between domestic public debt and growth across all samples. Moreover, the shares of domestic public debt appear to have a positive and statistically significant impact on growth in middle-income countries in specifications reported in columns 3 and 5 on table 4. In contrast, we observed an indirect link through the negative and significant impact of the interaction term between the domestic debt shares and financial development indicators (regressions 7 and 8, on table 5) in a sample of low income countries, implying that the combination of financial development and development of domestic debt markets exerts an independent and long-run influence on growth. A possible interpretation of this result is that a higher reliance on domestic debt in low-income countries with a relatively developed financial sector might create a "crowding out effect". Otherwise stated, due to the lack of viable lending opportunities in relatively developed financial systems of low-income countries (which results in a fixed level of available credit), an increase in the share of public sector credit (domestic public debt) in the total credit extended by the financial system will automatically reduce the share of credit to the private sector, which negatively impacts growth.

Given that a total public debt is composed of external and domestic public debt components, our findings suggests that the concave relationship between total public debt and growth is driven by the concave relationship that exists between public external debt, and not by the domestic component of it. Otherwise stated, it appears that high levels of external public debt are associated with low per capita GDP growth rates, but that high levels of domestic public debt are not necessarily associated with low growth. This analysis implies that the debt structure is relevant to growth and emphasizes the importance of the financial development and development of the domestic bond markets to promote long-lasting growth.

However, in a sample of high-income countries, we observed, again, no direct independent and statistically significant impact at conventional levels of both domestic and external public debt accumulation on growth by including separate debt shares as well as by including interaction terms (table 3). Consequently, per capita GDP growth is not sensitive to further public debt accumulation in given subset.

Estimating equation (2) does not alter any of the aforementioned temporal patterns. Financial development positively affects growth in the middle and low-income countries. This effects are especially robust to including different combinations of explanatory variables and the use of diverse estimation techniques in the middle-income countries. Hence, the low-income countries with low levels of financial development experience very little growth acceleration from a marginal increase in financial development. Again, high inflation has a statistically significant long-run negative impact on growth for the middle-income countries in all specifications reported on table 4. In the rest of subsamples, the coefficient estimates for inflation are generally negative and also statistically significant in some observations (table 3 and 5).

Our findings also suggest, however, the different impact of trade openness on growth by subsamples. Openness to trade are particularly influential in promoting growth in the middle-income (table 4) countries. Indeed, there is fairly strong evidence that the effects of openness persist in the long-run. Namely, the long-run coefficient of 0.010 on trade openness (table 4) implies positive, significant and long-run impacts of openness on per capita GDP growth for the middle-income countries. Openness also has a positive impact on growth in the high-income group. In contrast, the impact of openness on growth is mainly negative (although not always statistically significant) in specifications reported on table 5 for the low-income countries.

Yet again, our findings provide support for the hypothesis that the quality of institutions is a relevant factor for long-term growth. In particular, the institutions variable, proxied by the composite risk index from ICRG, positively correlates with growth in middle and high-income countries and the coefficients are strongly statistically significant when we allow for country fixed effects as tables 3 and 4 highlight. We also verified the robust positive effect of a high savings rate on per capita GDP growth in middle-income countries (table 4).

1.5.3. Robustness Tests

To ensure that our results are not driven by the presence of outliers, we checked the robustness of our findings and investigated the estimated equations with a reduced sample where outliers are eliminated. We also verified if the relationship between debt and growth survives after dropping the variable, specifically controlling for institutional quality (ICRG index). According to our evidence, we did not get results that would change the benchmark case results from estimation of equations 1 and 2. Consequently, our results are robust to these consistency tests.

1.6. Conclusion

We examined the growth impact of public debt by controlling for the institutional environment in which the debt was issued. Our analysis distinguishes between the growth impact of domestic versus external public debt, focusing on the importance of domestic financing.

Summarizing the results of our analysis, we mark the main findings, which are as follows. Observed patterns emphasize the relevance of the public debt structure. Vulnerabilities arising from high shares of external debt pose a long-term risk to growth. The incidence of public debt buildups is about the same for middle-income and low-income economies. In particular, the regressions' outcome points clearly in the direction of a non-linear relationship between total public debt-to-GDP and per capita GDP growth variables in the subsets of middle and low-income counties, and this relationship is mainly driven by the non-linear relationship that exists between public external debt and growth, and not by the domestic component of it. Otherwise stated, it appears that high levels of external public debt are associated with low per capita GDP growth rates, but that high levels of domestic public debt are not necessarily associated with low growth. We identified ranges of values for the optimal level of public debt (i.e. the level after which the marginal impact of further debt accumulation becomes harmful for growth). It also should be noted that high burdens of external public debt are likely owed to weak institutional structures and problematic political systems that make external borrowing a useful device for governments of developing countries to avoid hard fiscal policy decisions about spending and taxing. Yet, we did not find any support for a non-linear relationship between public debt and growth for high-income countries. This result is particularly remarkable, because it would suggest that high public debt levels for high-income countries are not necessarily associated with lower growth rates.

The analysis of the macroeconomic consequences of public debt accumulation is closely related to the debate on the sustainability of public finances. In fact, we give only a one-sided picture of debt-growth nexus, since comprehensive data on other sources of vulnerabilities associated with debt buildups that depend on the composition of the debt itself, which are maturity and currency mismatches, are much scarcer across countries and time.

Another noteworthy insight that emerged from the regressions output is a strong link between financial development and growth for the subset of middle-income countries. Our analysis implies that the domestic versus external public financing is relevant to growth and highlights the importance of the development of the domestic bond markets to promote long-lasting economic growth. It also suggests, however, that openness to trade and financial development are most influential in promoting growth in middle-income countries, whereas the impact of these two factors is relatively weak in low-income countries.

In light of the recent financial and economic crisis that has put explicit strains on public debt, the good debt management should be considered as clear priority for the financial stability and economic development. In terms of public policy implications, our findings suggest that the politicians ought to adopt policies that promote adjustment for optimal debt structure and that reduce the risk of sovereign finance by limiting excessive foreign borrowing and by developing the required institutional framework to foster financial sector development and expansion of the domestic bond market. Development of safer debt instruments can also help in reducing vulnerabilities and the probability of a debt crisis.

Chapter 2

PUBLIC DEBT STRUCTURE VERSUS FINANCIAL DEVELOPMENT

ABSTRACT

We investigated[1] the relation between public debt and financial development by controlling the macro and institutional factors in which the debt was issued in countries grouped by income levels for the period of 1994 to 2007. Our findings confirms that the development of a domestic debt market and reliance on domestic debt positively correlates with the level of financial development and macroeconomic stability, while it could have a complex interaction with the institutional framework. The results are robust across specifications and estimation strategies. The issue we address has not only a theoretical but also a policy relevance.

2.1. INTRODUCTION

In the first chapter, we have identified a strong link between financial development and economic growth across a subset of middle-income countries. Our analysis also highlighted the relevance of the debt structure and the development of the domestic bond markets to promote long-lasting economic growth. There are various strands of literature that have examined the effects of financial deepening and public debt on economic growth for

[1] I thank the participants of the seminar held at the University of Milan (Ph.D student seminar, November 2009) for helpful comments and suggestions.

different groups of countries. However, the interaction between financial development and public debt structure, in particular domestic versus external debt, remains largely unexplored in the literature. How do domestic debt markets interact with financial development? What is the impact of institutional factors on the development of domestic bond markets for countries at diverse stages of development? Our empirical work aims to address these issues through the application of panel data analysis. This allows us to investigate the nexus between public debt and financial development by controlling for macro and institutional factors in countries grouped by income levels for the period 1994-2007. We have also studied whether financial development has caused changes in debt composition and whether it has created a pledge against inflation, and vice versa. Our results provide strong evidence that financial sector development plays a key role in the development of the domestic debt market.

The chapter is organized as follows. The remainder of this section discusses the links among debt, finance and growth. The second section describes the data sources of the statistics, the methods and indicators of financial development we adopt and presents some stylized facts. The third and fourth sections discuss the empirical strategy and report econometric estimates for the debt-finance nexus, distinguishing among different subsamples and differing country characteristics. The paper concludes with the fifth section.

The link between economic growth and finance was studied by King and Levine (1993), Rajan and Zingales (1998), Levine (1999, 2003, 2005), DemirgüÇ-Kunt, A. and R. Levine (2001). This research provides evidence that financial sector development plays a role in growth. Moreover, Levine (1996) argues that the level of financial development is a good predictor of future rates of economic growth, capital accumulation, and technological change. There is also an opposing view based on Joan Robinson's (1952) claim that "finance follows"[2]. The results from studies by Allen et al., (2006) suggest that financial structures develop and prevail in response to the financial needs of firms and, as a consequence, to the characteristics of the real economy.

Given that a growing body of empirical analysis demonstrates a strong positive link between the functioning of the financial system and economic growth, other studies have focused on what determines financial development.

[2] In this interpretation the structure of the economy determines the types of intermediaries that are best suited to industrial firms. Hence, finance responds to changing demands from the "real sector".

In examining the determinants of financial system development La Porta et al., (1998) emphasize that a country's legal origins[3] are the central driving factor for financial development, as legal systems differ in their treatment of creditors and shareholders, and in contract enforcement. They showed that common law countries with greater shareholders' rights had relatively larger financial markets. Beck et al., (2003) suggest that a country's legal system is important for financial development because legal traditions differ in their ability to adapt efficiently to evolving economic conditions. Other studies find a positive relationship between per capita income and various indices of investor protection (Acemoglu, Johnson and Robinson, 2000) and suggest that legal origin has persistent, long-term effects on financial development. Ergungor (2004) investigates how the structure of a financial system – whether it is bank or market oriented – affects economic performance and presents evidence that civil law financial systems are more bank-oriented than common law financial systems. He argued that countries grow faster when they have a flexible judicial system and a more market – oriented financial system. There are also arguments in favor of growth-enhancing role of well-developed banks[4]. The structural theories have been criticized as incomplete to explain variations and differences in financial development we observe today. These theories emphasize the strong role of institutions and interest groups on financial development (Rajan and Zingales, 2003; Mayer and Sussman, 2001). Without dismissing the role of institutions, Levine (1999) advocates a functional approach to understand the role of financial systems in economic growth. His approach focuses on the ties between growth and the quality of the functions provided by the financial system. Indeed, as Levine, Loayza and Beck (1999) findings suggest, the legal and accounting reforms that strengthen creditor rights, contract enforcement, and accounting practices boost financial development and accelerate economic growth.

Monetary and fiscal policies may also affect the provision of financial services (Bencivenga and Smith, 1992, Roubini and Sala-i-Martin, 1992, 1995). The effects of inflation on financial development were examined by Huybens and Smith (1999) and Boynd, Levine and Smith (2001). Their research showed that economies with higher inflation rates are more likely to

[3] Legal systems originate from a limited number of legal traditions: English Common Law and French, German and Scandinavian Civil Law. Figure 2 shows a world map of Legal Origin.

[4] From this perspective banks do not suffer from the same fundamental shortcomings as markets. Thus, they will do a correspondingly better job at researching firms, overseeing managers, and financing industrial expansion. This will result a better resource allocation and economic performance.

have smaller, less active, and less efficient banks and equity markets. Depending on the currency composition of the debt, its real value could be reduced with higher inflation and currency depreciation.

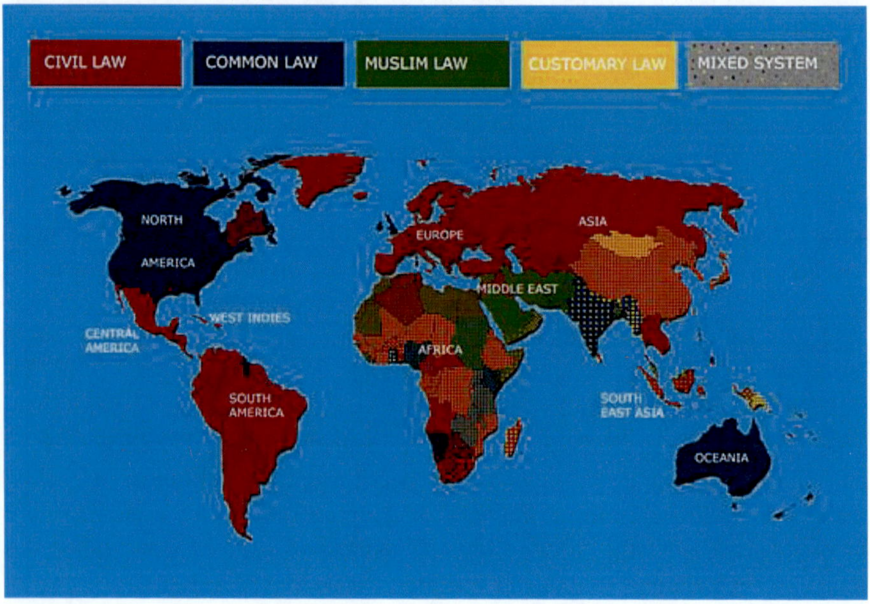

Figure 2. Legal Origin – World Map[5].

The importance of the composition of public debt for the government's ability to maintain its anti-inflation stance was studied by Missale and Blanchard (1991). They suggest that, at high levels of debt, the government may need to decrease the maturity of the debt in order to signal an anti-inflationary commitment. As Guscina (2008) pointed out, an unstable macroeconomic environment, poor quality institutions, and an uncertain political climate hinder the development of domestic debt markets, while low levels of inflation, openness, transparency and fairness in government funding operations, as well as a strong legal system, create a favorable environment for development.

The role of trade openness to promote financial development was explored by Rajan and Zingales (2003) and Huang and Temple (2005). Their research, that excludes transition countries, suggests that financial development is higher in countries that are more open to trade. Quy-Toan Do and Levchenko

[5] Source: http://www.juriglobe.ca/eng/index.php

(2004) explained how trade openness affects in non linear way the financial systems of countries. They noted that, while in advanced economies trade promotes financial systems, it has an opposite effect in low income countries. Chin and Ito (2006) studied the effects of capital account liberalization on financial development and found that financial openness matters only when a threshold level of legal and institutional development has been attained. While this broad spectrum of work suggests that the direct laws, regulations and macroeconomic policies shape the financial system, there are studies that also suggest that political, cultural and even geographic context influences the financial system (Haber (2004); Haber, Maurer and Razo (2003); Guiso, Sapienza, and Zingales (2004); Stulz and Williamson (2003); Easterly and Levine (2003)). However, the extent to which financial development and creation of a domestic debt market interact is constrained by a lack of comprehensive empirical studies.

Our analysis takes into account existing studies and tests for how financial development impacts the composition of the public debt by controlling for macroeconomic fundamentals, enforcement capacity of the governments and institutional factors. We focus on the share of domestic debt in total debt as a proxy for the development of domestic debt market.

2.2. The Data and Stylized Facts

The econometric study covers the period between 1994-2007 and distinguishes countries by their income levels. In particular, in this study we employed samples that are more likely to be homogenous by splitting the countries into high-income, middle income and low-income groups[6].

The data are from various sources. To capture the composition of public debt, we used the dataset introduced by Panizza (2008) covering up to 130 countries for the period of 1994-2007. The dataset consists of: Domestic, External and Total public debt data[7]. To capture the composition of the debt we considered the ratio of domestic debt-to-total debt. The other debt ration we employed is the ratio of total debt-to-GDP. To proxy for institutions we used “Law and Order”, “Quality of bureaucracy”, “Government stability” and

[6] The list of countries are reported on Appendix I. The split among high-income, middle-income and low-income countries is made along the WB classification.

[7] Public debt classification includes: Central government debt, general government and non-financial public sector debt.

"Composite Political, Financial, and Economic Risk Rating[8]" from the International Country Risk Guide (ICRG). Other macroeconomic variables such as inflation (measured as annual growth rates of the consumer price index), Real Exchange rate volatility (std. deviation) over the last 5 years, Savings rate, Trade openness[9] come from the World Development Indicators Database published by the World Bank.

We used annual data for the period of 1994-2007 from "The New Database on Financial Development and Structure (2010)" by Thorsten Beck, Asli Demirguc-Kunt and Ross Eric Levine for the indicators of financial development, which are as follows[10]: i) the ratio of liquid liabilities (LLY) of the financial system to GDP (currency plus demand and interest-bearing liabilities of bank and nonbank financial intermediaries)[11]; ii) the ratio of credit issued to the private sector by banks and other financial intermediaries to GDP (PRIVO); iii) the ratio of commercial bank assets to the sum of commercial bank assets and central bank assets (BTOT). To measure the efficiency of the financial intermediation, we made use of the following variables: the ratio of overhead costs (OVC) to total bank assets[12] and Net Interest Margin (NIM), the difference between bank interest income and interest expenses, divided by total assets[13]. For a more specific view of financial development, we employed indicators such as: i) stock market turnover (TOR), the ratio of trades in domestic shares to market capitalization[14], to evaluate financial sector efficiency or sophistication; ii) market capitalization (MCAP) relative to GDP; iii) Total value traded (TVT), the ratio of trades in domestic shares (on domestic exchanges) to GDP as indicators of stock market activity.

---

[8] The index rises as the risk reduces and stability increases. It can be used as a proxy for institutional quality as good institutions affect risk and stability.

[9] Index suggested by Rajan and Zingales (2003), i.e. the sum of exports and imports of goods and services as a share of GDP.

[10] The description mainly follows Demirguc-Kunt and Levine (1996, 1999).

[11] This indicator roughly corresponds to M2/GDP and was first used by McKinnon (1973) and King and Levine (1993) among others.

[12] In the short run, high overhead costs may be related to investments by competitive banks in improving financial services, but over a longer time period, high overhead costs are likely to reflect inefficiency and lack of competition.

[13] High values for this variable tend to suggest a lack of competition among banks.

[14] High values of TOR indicate a more active equity market, which may be associated with a relatively efficient allocation of capital.

Table 3. Descriptive Statistics: 1994-2007

a. Summary Statistics: Debt and observed Financial Development measure

Variable	Observation	Mean	Std. Dev.	Min	Max
LLY	2254	0.5233362	0.4204615	0.0019442	4.317595
PRIVO	2271	0.4488132	0.425063	0.0011415	2.697557
BTOT	2486	0.8163509	0.2155358	0.0173321	1.264457
MCAP	1488	0.5136265	0.6139286	0.0002124	6.034795
BTOT	2486	0.8163509	0.2155358	0.0173321	1.264457
OVC	2105	0.0447761	0 .0292232	0.0017692	0.2697982
NIM	2071	0.0522774	0.0371445	0.0036907	0.4204413
TVT	1497	0.3254365	0.6322727	0	5.411863
TOR	1524	0.4685399	0.8127776	0	16.78062
Totaldebt/gdp	1910	0.6327807	0.5322461	0	6.7
Domest./Total debt	1673	0.3948202	0.289128	0	1.043144

b. Correlation matrix: Debt and observed Financial Development measures

LLY		PRIVO	BTOT	OVC	NIM	MCAP	TVT	TOR	TD/GDP DD/TD
LLY	1.0000								
PRIVO	0.0377	1.0000							
BTOT	0.0527	0.5028	1.0000						
OVC	-0.4562	-0.4410	-0.3864	1.0000					
NIM	-0.4996	-0.5192	-0.4277	0.7022	1.0000				
MCAP	0.6073	0.6366	0.3300	-0.2632	-0.2608	1.0000			
TVT	0.3679	0.5840	0.2549	-0.2195	-0.2625	0.6778	1.0000		
TOR	0.0557	0.2114	0.1019	-0.1024	-0.1286	0.1591	0.5139	1.0000	
TD/GD	-0.1133	-0.2063	-0.4710	0.1128	0.1588	-0.0874	-0.1351	-0.1072	1.0000
DD/TD	0.5576	0.6288	0.4568	-0.4108	-0.4577	0.4710	0.4063	0.2426	-0.0847 1.0000

Table 4. Constructed Indicators of Financial Development

a. PCA results

Measure	Eigenvalue	Proportion	LLY	PRIVO	BTOT	OVC	NIM	MCAP	TVT	TOR
FD	4.7	0.59	0.40	0.41	0.28	-0.34	-0.37	0.35	0.37	0.28
FDSIZE	1.6	0.80	0.70					0.70		
FDEFF	2.5	0.63				-0.48	-0.50		0.54	0.48
FDBANK	3.38	0.68	0.49	0.48	0.34	-0.44	-0.47			
FDSTOCK	2.31	0.77						0.52	0.66	0.54
FDEPTH	2.17	0.72	0.58	0.51	0.63					

b. Correlation matrix: Debt and Constructed Indicators of Financial Development

FD		FDSIZE	FDEFF	FDBANK	FDSTOCK	FDEPTH	TD/GDP	DD/TD
FD	1.0000							
FDSIZE	0.9062	1.0000						
FDEFF	0.9298	0.7342	1.0000					
FDBANK	0.9424	0.8488	0.8400	1.0000				
FDSTOCK	0.8193	0.7299	0.8557	0.5846	1.0000			
FDEPTH	0.9263	0.8657	0.7496	0.9364	0.5874	1.0000		
TD/GDP	-0.1548	-0.0264	-0.1151	-0.2547	-0.1010	-0.3436	1.0000	
DD/GDP	0.7088	0.6553	0.6396	0.6486	0.6081	0.6022	-0.0847	1.0000

Table 3 presents the Descriptive Statistics for the whole sample. On "Panel a" we present "Summary Statistics" for debt and observed financial development measures. On "Panel b" we present the correlation matrix between debt and observed financial development measures.

To produce new aggregate indices for financial development based on the described variables, we used principal component analysis (PCA)[1]. The PCA takes N specific indicators and produces new indices (the principal components) $X_1, X_2,...X_N$ that are mutually uncorrelated. Each principal component, as a linear combination of the N indicators, captures a different dimension of the data. The variances of several of the principal components are low enough to be negligible, and, therefore, most of the variation in the data is captured by a small number of indices. Based on this methodology, the first principal component, defined by a vector of weights $\alpha=(\alpha_1, \alpha_2,...,\alpha_N)'$ on the (standardized) indicators $X=(X_1, X_2,...X_n)'$, accounts for the greatest amount of the variation in the original set of indicators in the sense that the linear combination, αX, corresponding to the first principal components, has the highest sample variance for any possible weights, subject to the constraint that the sum-of-squares of the weights placed on each existing indicator is equal to one: $\alpha'\alpha=1$.

Table 4, "Panel a" reports the structures of constructed indicators of financial development for whole sample. In particular, the table shows the following: the eigenvalues, proportion explained, and the eigenvector (coefficients of the standardized variables) of each first principal component from which the new indicators of financial development are defined. The first principal component is the linear combination of the measures selected. The eigenvalues are the variances of the (first) principal components.

The first indicators of overall financial development (FD) are constructed from eight components, namely, Liquid Liabilities (LLY), Private Credit (PRIVO), Commercial Bank assets (BTOT), Overhead Cost (OVC), Net Interest Margin (NIM), Stock market Capitalization (MCAP), Stock market Value Traded (TVT) and Turnover Ratio (TOR). For whole sample the first principal component accounts for 59% of the variation in these eight indicators. The weights from PCA analysis are 0.40 for LLY, 0.41 for PRIVO, 0.28 for BTOT, -0.34 for OVC, -0.37 for NIM, 0.35 for MCAP, 0.37 for TVT and 0.28 for TOR. Hence, the negative correlations between the OVC and NIM and aggregate indicators of financial sector development are observed, demonstrating that high values for these indicators point toward inefficiency in

[1] Based on the approach of Huang and Temple (2005).

the financial sector, while the rest of the variables have positive correlations with aggregate indicators of financial sector development. The measure, FDSIZE, is constructed from LLY and MCAP and captures the size of a financial system[2]. The first principal component accounts for 80% of the variation in these two measures. FDEFF, which accounts for 63% of the total variation in these indicators, captures financial efficiency, and OVC, NIM, TVT and TOR variables are used to construct it. Lower values of this index indicate a higher level of financial sector efficiency or sophistication. The measure, FDBANK, captures the extent of bank-based intermediation. It uses LLY, PRIVO, BTOT, OVC and NIM and accounts for 68% of the variation in these five indicators. FDSTOK is a measure of stock market development and accounts for 77% of the variation in MCAP, TVT and TOR. Lastly, the measure of financial depth, FDEPTH, is developed from three underlying series - LLY, PRIVO and BTOT and accounts for 72% of the variation in these indicators for sample as a whole. With private sector credit included to construct the index, the letter's response to "Domestic Debt-to-Total Debt ratio" would also shed light on any crowding out effects.

Table 4, "Panel b" presents a correlation matrix among debt and constructed indicators of financial development for the whole sample. Constructed indicators are highly correlated with one another, as we predicted. The correlations between debt and the constructed indicators are still low, but higher than when the original proxies are used under the theory that aggregation of the original measures reduces measurement error. The lowest correlation was detected between FDBANK and FDSTOCK (0.58), reflecting the type of intermediation that is either bank or stock market-oriented. Definitions and data sources for all variables used in the empirical analysis are reported on Table 1.

Figure 3 plots the financial depth trends by income group and shows the effects of the medium extent of financial development (measured by financial depth indexed) for "High income: OECD", "High income: non OECD", "Upper middle income", "Lower middle income" and "Low income countries". To observe the relationship between domestic debt and financial development indicators, we have employed scatter plots. Figures 4 through 7 plot financial development (measured by BTOT, PRIVO, FD and FDEPTH) against "Domestic Debt-to-Total Debt." We find strong evidence that financial development and domestic debt shares are related. The evidence lends some

[2] Provides a summary of the combined importance of bank-based and equity-based finance, relative to GDP.

support to the notion that macroeconomic and political stability as well as the quality of institutions are crucial to the development of a domestic debt market (Guscina, 2008).

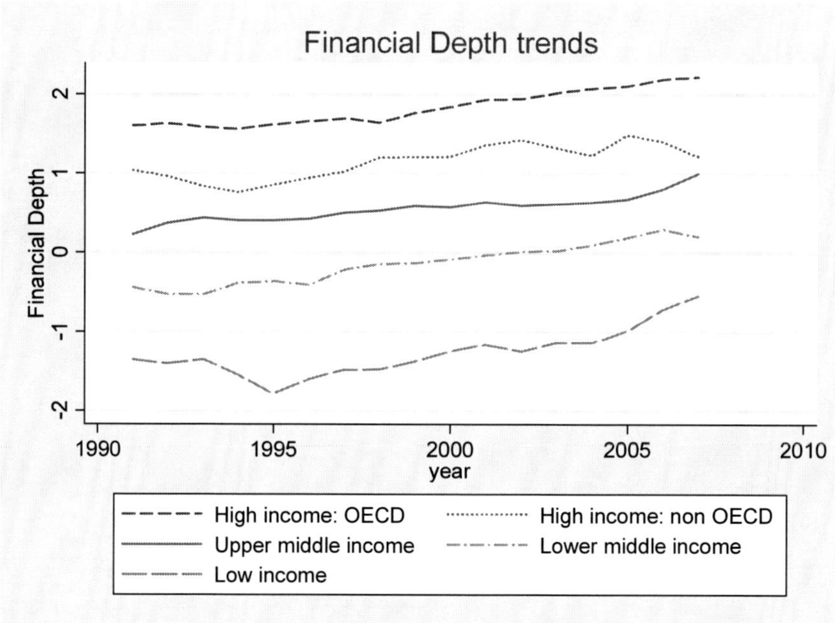

Figure 3. Financial Depth Trends by income group.

2.3. THE EMPIRICAL FRAMEWORK

The econometric analysis covers the time period between 1994 and 2007. The countries included in the sample are classified by their income levels based on WB income group classification[3] and are grouped into three groups. The groups consist of: High income, Middle income and Low income countries.

The high income group includes: "High income: OECD" and "High income: non OECD" countries; The middle income group includes: "Upper middle income" and "Lower middle income" countries, while the low income group includes: "Low income" countries as classified in the WB database.

---

[3] WB classification includes: High income: OECD, High income: non OECD, Upper middle income, Lower middle income and Low income countries.

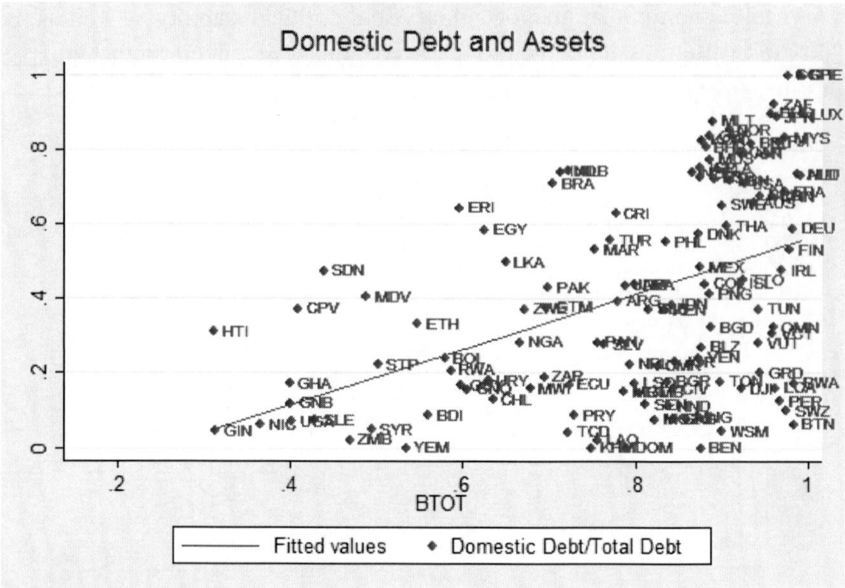

Figure 4. Domestic Debt/Total Debt Vs. Financial Development (measured by BTOT) for the whole sample.

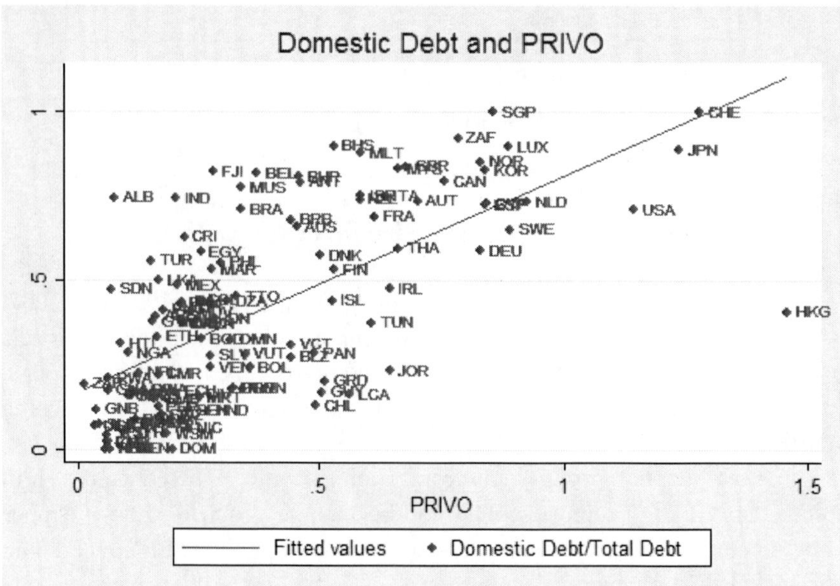

Figure 5. Domestic Debt/Total Debt vs. Financial Development (measured by PRIVO) for the whole sample.

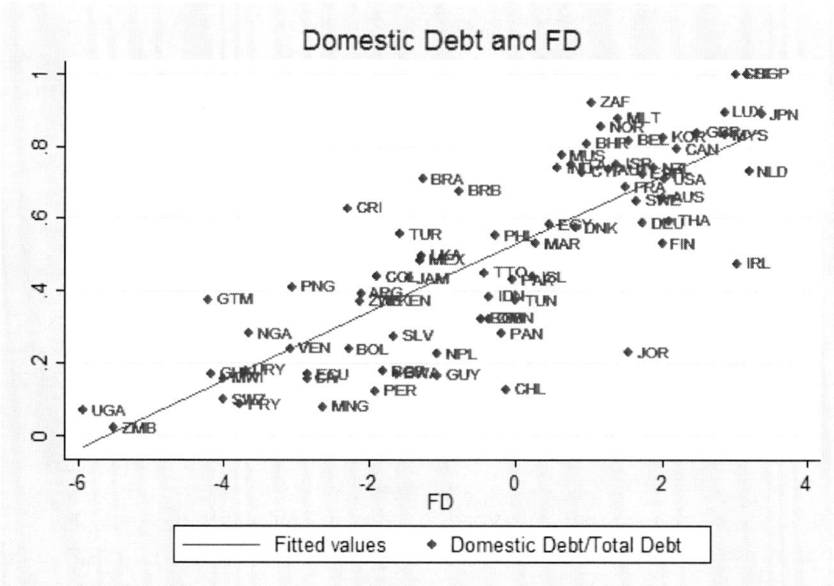

Figure 6. Domestic Debt/Total Debt vs. Financial Development (measured by FD) for the whole sample.

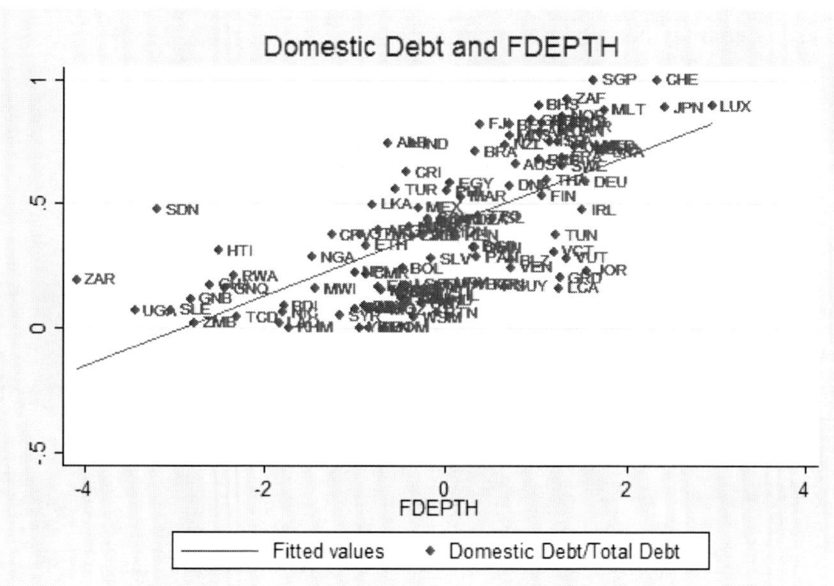

Figure 7. Domestic Debt/Total Debt vs. Financial Development (measured by FDEPTH) for the whole sample.

To investigate the determinants of the share of domestic debt in total debt, we analyzed the factors influencing on a country's ability to issue domestic debt and considered the Level of Financial Development, Law and Order, Quality of Bureaucracy, Government Stability, ICRG Composite Risk Rating, Exchange Rate Volatility, Savings Rate, Openness to Trade, Total Debt-to-GDP Ratio, and Inflation as explanatory variables and Domestic Debt-to-Total Debt Ratio as the dependent variable. To proxy for financial development, different measures and constructed indicators of financial development (described above) were chosen.

Since macroeconomic instability is likely to undermine the development of a domestic debt market, high inflation and exchange rate volatility should have a negative impact on domestic debt accumulation. Conversely, a higher level of financial development as well as a higher savings rate and more openness to trade are expected to enhance the domestic debt issuance. The institutional framework could have a complex interaction with domestic debt. Countries with strong domestic institutions are better able to raise funds domestically. Investors view such countries as having a competent policy framework and a commitment to law and order. Furthermore, these countries can generally be relied upon to preserve property rights and optimally use fiscal resources for the provision of public services. However, the issuance of domestic debt may be less important in stable institutional environments as the collateral or risk diversification function that a given type of debt performs on banks' balance sheets will play a smaller role once the overall magnitude of risk in the economy is low. Hence, in our sample of high income countries, defining *a priori* which of the two effects outweighs (complement or substitute effect of good institutions to the process of domestic debt issuance) is not apparent.

In studying the link between financial development and public debt we exploited 3 alternative approaches to capture various aspects of public indebtedness, financial development and institutional quality. First, we estimated the following general equation to investigate the (linear) effects of debt accumulation with the Country Fixed Effects (FE) method:

$$DDebt_{it} = \alpha_i + \varphi_1 X_{it} + \varphi_2 FD_{it} + \xi_{it} \qquad (1)$$

where $DDebt_{it}$ denotes country i's (i = 1, . . . , N) Domestic Debt-to-Total Debt Ratio in year t; X_{it} denotes a vector of control variables (which varies across specifications) with unknown weights φ_1; FD_{it} is the indicator of financial development in year t; α_i captures time invariant country components and ε_{it} represent the usual disturbance terms. We relaxed identically-distributed-errors assumptions by assuming that disturbances (unmeasured influences on the dependent variable) were correlated within the countries. Viewing each country as a cluster[4] should yield more realistic standard errors and confidence intervals estimates.

Recognizing that financial development is potentially endogenous and correlated with the unobserved country effects, we employed a second approach based on Simultaneous Equations Model (SEM) and estimated the following general two-equation system in panel data context:

$$\begin{aligned} DDebt_{it} &= \alpha_{i1} + \varphi_1 FD_{it} + \varphi_2 X_{it1} + \varphi_3 Z_{it} + \xi_{it1} \\ FD_{it} &= \alpha_{i2} + \varphi_4 DDebt_{it} + \varphi_5 X_{it2} + \varphi_6 W_{it} + \xi_{it2} \end{aligned} \quad (2)$$

where $DDebt_{it}$ and FD are endogenous variables, $DDebt_{it}$ denotes country i's (i = 1, . . . , N) Domestic Debt-to-Total Debt Ratio in year t; FD_{it} denotes country i's (i = 1, . . . , N) indicator of financial development in year t; X_{it1} or X_{it2} denotes a set of exogenous explanatory variables (which vary across specifications) in each equation with unknown weights φ_2 and φ_5. In some cases, X_{it1} and X_{it2} may overlap.

We imposed exclusion restrictions on the model by assuming that W_{it} and Z_{it} are vectors of exogenous variables such that W_{it} do not appear in the first equation and Z_{it} is absent from the second equation; The instrumental variables consist of the exogenous variables appearing in either equation, so we can use Z_{it} to instrument DDebt and W_{it} to instrument FD; ξ are the structural error terms.

Since dependent variables show high persistence, as the final feature, we considered a model of the Domestic Debt as a share of total debt depending on the prior year's value (the set of right hand side variables now includes the lagged dependent variable) along with the other control variables. We provided a set of instruments for the model and estimated the dynamic panel data equation with country-specific effects:

$$DDebt_{it} = \alpha_i + \varphi_1 DDebt_{it-1} + \varphi_2 X_{it} + \varphi_3 FD_{it} + \xi_{it} \quad (3)$$

where $DDebt_{it}$ denotes a Domestic Debt-to-Total Debt Ratio in year t, FD_{it} (measure of financial development) and X_{it} (which varies across

[4] Adding the option cluster (cncode) to a regression command yields robust standard errors across clusters defined by cncode (country code).

specifications) will be a set of control variables. The presence of dynamics in this approach is a major change for the purpose of interpreting the model. With the lagged dependent variable, we now have in the equation the entire history of the right hand side variables.

Consequently, any measured influence is conditioned on this history. However, the Country Fixed Effects (FE) model cannot deal with endogenous regressors (a key concern in the present context) and is biased and inconsistent in dynamic panel data models of the type we are estimating, while the Simultaneous Equations Model cannot accommodate country-specific fixed effects. For these reasons, we rely on GMM[5] estimation of our regressions, designed for dynamic "small-T, large-N" panels that may contain fixed effects and, separate from those fixed effects, idiosyncratic errors that are heteroskedastic and correlated within but not across countries. Hence, GMM specification allows us to identify the model in an optimal fashion. It can exploit a panel structure of the model, easily accommodate country-specific fixed effects, and provide a set of instruments for the model as in the Simultaneous Equation Model.

In addition, GMM specification is more robust to misspecification (because we only need a specific equation for domestic debt-to-total debt ratio) and allows for the lagged dependent variable to accommodate realistic dynamics (persistent dependent variable).

Our specification includes the original GMM estimator[6] and the "two-step" version of the expanded estimator[7] with "Windmeijer finite-sample correction" to the standard errors. We calculated a point estimate for the long-run effect[8] of financial development on domestic debt share in total debt: $\beta_{LR}=\beta/(1-\varphi)$, where β is the coefficient of interest on a measure of financial development estimated in the regression and φ is the coefficient on the lagged dependent variable, to examine whether increases in financial development are followed by increases in domestic debt share in total debt, and whether this effect persists into the long run.

The results of the Country Fixed Effects (FE) model, Simultaneous Equations models (SEM) and GMM Estimation of our regressions are reported in Appendixes III through V.

---

[5] "GMM" stands for Generalized Method of Moments.

[6] Available in STATA as *xtabond* option.

[7] Available in STATA with *xtabond2* option (Roodman (2006)).

[8] Available in STATA with "nlcom" option, which takes nonlinear combination of the estimated coefficients and computes standard errors using the delta method.

2.4. Determinants of the Ratio of Domestic Debt-to-Total Debt

In studying the determinants of the ratio of domestic debt-to-total debt, we start from a simple model and follow a procedure of changing explanatory variables. To avoid multicolinearity problems in multivariate regressions, one proxy is chosen from each set of the explanatory variables, capturing different features of financial development and, thus, operating through different channels. The FE regression results are reported in Appendix III for the whole sample (by subsamples), while the SEM results are reported in Appendix IV, and GMM results are reported in Appendix V.

Beginning with financial development measures, the results, for the most part, show that the share of domestic debt in total debt positively depends on the level of financial development. The results hold across subsamples, are robust, and include either different combinations of explanatory variables or diverse estimation techniques. There is a much stronger impact for the middle income subsample than for the rest of the subsamples. In particular, the level of financial development measures, such as LLY, BTOT and MCAP, always have positive and, predominantly, statistically high significant effects on the domestic debt-to-total debt variable for the middle income subsample. Hence, changes in liquid liabilities (LLY) of the financial system's ratio to GDP have a large, positive and significant effect on middle income countries. The range for the coefficient was between 0. 667 with SEM (Appendix IV, table 1), 0.379 for FE (Appendix III, table 2) and 0.184 for GMM (Appendix V, table 1). Taking 0.38 as the average, increasing LLY by one standard deviation (0.28), implies an increase of 0.11 in the domestic debt-to-total debt ratio. Furthermore, there is fairly strong evidence that the effect of financial development (measured by LLY) persists into the long-run. Specifically, the long-run effect of LLY on the domestic debt share in total debt gives a coefficient of 0.492 (significant at the 5% level), meaning that a one standard deviation (0.28) increase in LLY is associated with an increase of 0.138 in domestic debt-to-total debt ratio. The results on BTOT indicate that the countries with a larger share of private banks' assets in total banks' assets appear to issue more domestic debt. This may indicate that more developed banking systems create demand for government securities. Although, the higher ratio of stocks traded (MCAP) relative to GDP associated with a higher share of domestic debt in total debt, suggests that stock market development is correlated with higher reliance on domestic debt.

The impact of PRIVO on domestic debt-to-total debt ratio for middle income countries is negative in a number of SEM estimations, and some coefficients are highly statistically significant (table 3, Appendix IV). One possible explanation is that a higher reliance on domestic debt in a country with a better developed banking sector might create a "crowding out effect" on private credit allocation and reduce the size of private banking. Likewise, the variable of private credit to GDP ratio may well include nonperforming loans to the private sector. The observed effect on PRIVO is consistent with those obtained by Guscina (2008) and Hauner (2008). On the other hand, in case of a higher share of commercial banks in the banking sector, they might be less willing to absorb public debt. It should also be noted that the observed effect is not robust and SEM estimation doesn't completely deal with the bias caused by the endogeneity of the control variables.

In the high income subsample, the SEM result, which showed a statistically significant and positive association between LLY and domestic debt-to-total debt (coefficient on LLY is equal 0.163, Appendix IV, table 1), practically disappears once fixed effects are included (coefficients equal 0.058, as shown in regression 1, or -0.069, as shown in regression 4, on table 2, Appendix III and are not statistically significant) as well as in the case of GMM (coefficient equals -0.093 as shown in regression 1, table 1 or -0.140, as shown in regression 1, table 4, Appendix V and are not statistically significant). For this reason, the SEM correlation is primarily coming from unobserved time-invariant differences in the sample of high income countries. The effect of BTOT is positive in all estimation types, suggesting that the size of the private banking sector positively correlates with the reliance on domestic debt, although the effect is highly statistically significant in GMM estimation. However, the credit issued to the private sector by banks and other financial intermediaries to GDP Ratio (PRIVO) has a negative but not statistically significant coefficient in some FE and SEM specifications, while the effect is always positive and significant in our preferred GMM estimation when the bias caused by endogeneity of "crowding out effect" disappears. In economic terms, this implies that the association between government debt and the size of bank loans to the private sector is not necessarily negative or, in other words, a higher reliance on domestic debt does not necessarily create a crowding out effect on private credit allocation, save for a developed and highly competitive financial sector. We cannot support the results of De Bonis et al., (2009), which suggest that there is a negative link between government debt and the credit granted by the banking system to the private sector, relative to GDP in industrialized countries. However, in the case of high income countries, the positive and, in some cases, statistically significant effect of the stock market capitalization variable (MCAP) on domestic debt-to-total debt ratio is observed only after including a set of instruments for endogenous variables in the model (SEM and GMM specifications). No significant effect of measures of lower stages of financial development in the case of high income countries could be due to the fact that these countries had already reached the stage of development of their financial sector when other indicators are more relevant. Moreover, the mentioned financial indicators do not carry major weight for the time period of 1994 to 2007.

We also tested whether the impact of financial development on the domestic debt share is statistically significant for the low income countries subsample. The results suggest that a higher level of financial development allows these countries to issue more domestic debt. In particular, we observed a positive and, for most specifications, statistically significant effect of the level of financial development measured by LLY and BTOT on the domestic-to-total debt variable. The long-run effect of LLY on domestic debt share in total debt gives a coefficient of 1.122 (Appendix V, table 4) and is very precisely estimated (P=0.007), meaning that a one standard deviation (0.134) increase in LLY causes long-run increase of domestic debt-to-total debt ratio by 0.15. A positive and statistically significant effect of PRIVO was observed only in FE and SEM estimations, while the effect of PRIVO was negative in the GMM estimation, which deals with the bias caused by endogeneity. The negative relationship between domestic debt share in total public debt and financial development (measured by PRIVO) may be due to the lack of viable lending opportunities[9] in poorly developed financial systems. The ability of low income countries to expand domestic debt without reducing the loans to the private sector, to some extent, depends on the importance of financial intermediaries (pension funds, insurance companies, etc.) in the institutional framework of a country. The presence of competition in the financial sector on the government securities market can smooth the typical crowding out effect.

Coming to macroeconomic instability, the inflation rate always has a negative and, for the most part, statistically significant coefficient for the high income subsample. This result is robust regardless of the different combinations of explanatory variables considered, suggesting that in advanced economies low and stable inflation is associated with higher domestic debt share in total public debt. By contrast, inflation appears to not affect the

[9] For a given fixed level of available bank credit, an increase in the share of public sector credit (domestic public debt) in the total credit extended by the commercial banking system will automatically reduce the share of bank credit to the private sector to GDP.

domestic debt-to-total debt ratio for low and middle income countries. In some cases, the coefficient on inflation is even positive and significant at conventional levels, invoking to policy instruments such as debt inflation, thus leading to low cost of domestic funding. In the case of middle income countries we show that the negative impact of inflation is statistically significant when there are no other explanatory variables (table 1, Appendix III). Once we control for the level of financial development (LLY and MCAP), inflation loses its power to explain the ratio of domestic debt to total debt, whereas financial development variables remain almost always significant. This nexus points toward the hypothesis that low inflation could be associated with financial development.

The coefficients of total debt-to-GDP only in some specifications have a negative impact on domestic debt-to-total debt ratios in the whole sample, reflecting the fact that highly indebted countries would find it problematic to issue more domestic debt.

The institutional quality proxied by the ICRG composite risk index has a positive impact on countries' ability to issue domestic debt. This result confirms that the development of a domestic debt market and reliance on domestic debt is correlated with countries' composite risk rating. In other words, countries with a higher composite risk rating are better able to raise necessary funds domestically. The result is very robust and holds across subsamples. In high income countries an increase of one standard deviation (5.48) in the ICRG composite risk index is associated with an increase of 0.38 in domestic debt-to-total debt ratio, while in middle income countries an increase of one standard deviation (8.57) in the ICRG composite risk index is associated with an increase of 0.31 and in low income countries an increase of one standard deviation (9.39) in the ICRG composite risk index is associated with an increase of 0.35 in domestic debt-to-total debt ratio (FE specification, Appendix III, table 3). The coefficient on Quality of Bureaucracy is positive, but it is significant only in a few regressions for middle and high income countries in GMM specification. Government Stability has a positive and, often, statistically significant effect in middle and low income countries, while the coefficients on Government stability are mostly negative in high income countries subset reflecting the prevalence of the substitution effect of good institutions to the process of domestic debt issuance. One possible explanation for the predominantly negative coefficient on the "Law and Order" variable could be the result of similar reasoning. Namely, the issuance of domestic debt may be less relevant in stable institutional environments since the collateral or risk diversification function that a given type of debt performs on banks' balance sheets will play a smaller role once the country has stable governance committed to law and order.

The coefficients on the lagged dependent variable (domestic debt share in total debt) is, expectedly, significant and positive in all GMM estimations hovering in the 0.6 to 0.8 range for high and middle income countries and 0.5 to 0.7 range for low income countries.

The coefficient on the Savings rate is mainly positive and statistically significant in FE and SEM estimations for middle and low income countries, while in GMM estimation, a negative and statistically significant coefficient is often observed for middle income countries. In high income countries the impact of the saving rate on the domestic debt share is mainly negative, although not always statistically significant, in all specifications. These results imply that higher savings rates in a globally integrated financial system do not necessarily translate into higher domestic debt share in total government debt.

The regression results from SEM estimation show a different impact of trade openness on the domestic debt shares across countries. While in high income countries trade openness has, generally, a positive impact, its effect is negative in middle and low income countries. A more open systems to trade are also more open financially, it is possible that these countries issue more foreign debt that is less risky because it is hedged by exports. However, trade openness has an unstable sign and is insignificant in most FE and GMM estimations in all subsamples. Moreover, a trade-to-GDP ratio, used as a measure of openness, is influenced by some underlying phenomenon, such as exchange rate fluctuations. Furthermore, an unstable monetary environment characterized by high exchange rate volatility is associated with a lower share of domestic debt in total debt, as was expected.

Finally, we estimated the effect of constructed indicators, which capture the different features of financial development (along with inflation, total debt-to-GDP, and macro and institutional indicators) on domestic debt-to-total debt ratios. Reassuringly, the consistently positive impact of financial development on the domestic debt-to-total debt ratio is also observed for principal component indicators across all estimation techniques. The regressions' results, reported in Appendix III through V, are robust and hold across subsamples.

The coefficients of FD, FDEPTH, FDEFF, FDSIZE, FDBANK are always positive in the middle income subsample and the effect is strongly statistically significant for most of the specifications. Constructed indicators are standardized, meaning that one standard deviation (2.01) increase in the index of overall financial development (FD) is associated with a 0.12 increase in the share of domestic debt, and one standard deviation (1.43) increase in the index of financial depth (FDEPTH) is associated with a 0.10 increase in the share of domestic debt for the middle income subsample (Appendix III, table 4). Furthermore, one standard deviation (1.71) increase in FDBANK (measuring the extent of bank based intermediation) is associated with a 0.11 increase in the share of domestic debt in total debt, and one standard deviation (1.24) increase in FDSIZE is associated with a 0.07 percentage points increase in the share of domestic debt in total debt for the middle income subsample.

The coefficients of FDEPTH cannot adequately explain the ratio of domestic debt-to-total debt for the low income subsample in almost all estimations, reflecting an underdeveloped financial sector. The coefficient on FDBANK (measuring the extent of bank based intermediation) is statistically significant only in SEM estimation. The coefficient on FDSIZE indicator is positive and statistically significant in the FE estimation, pointing toward a positive link between "financial size" of a country and the capacity of domestic debt issuance.

The regression results of GMM estimation for high income countries, based on constructed indicators, suggest the relevance of constructed indicators, especially when measuring a depth (FDEPTH) and efficiency (FDEFF) of financial intermediation. Hence, these indicators of financial development have a highly statistically significant impact on a country's ability to issue domestic debt.

2.5. Conclusion

Our results provide strong evidence that financial sector development plays a key role in the development of the domestic debt market. The domestic debt market is, in and of itself, an integral part of the process of financial development. The results indicate that the share of domestic debt in total debt positively depends on the level of financial development. That is, a higher level of financial development allows countries to issue more domestic debt in all country groups.

According to our results, the level of financial development as measured by liquid liabilities (LLY), by the share of commercial bank assets to total bank assets (BTOT) and by the stock market capitalization relative to GDP (MCAP) consistently has a strong positive impact on the share of domestic debt for the middle and low income subsamples, while the impact on changes in this indicators is stronger for middle income countries than for the rest of the subsamples. Another robust result that holds across subsamples indicates that the countries with larger shares of private banks in total bank assets (BTOT) appear to issue more domestic debt. This might reflect the fact that more developed banking systems may create demand for government securities. By contrast, in the case of high income countries as a group, we did not find an apparent contemporaneous relation between the share of domestic debt in total debt and financial development indicators such as liquid liabilities M2 to GDP (LLY), stock market capitalization relative to GDP (MCAP), dimension of the banking sector (FDBANK), stock market development measure (FDSTOCK), size of a financial system (FDSIZE) and overall financial development (FD). This could be due to the fact that advanced economies by 1994 had already reached the development of their financial sector, and observed indicators of lower stages of financial development did not carry major weight for the time period of 1994 to 2007. Simultaneously, our results show the importance of indicators measuring the depth (FDEPTH) and efficiency (FDEFF) of financial intermediation for a high-income country's ability to issue more domestic debt.

Unlike the results of previous research (De Bonis et al., 2009), the impact of the ratio of private sector credit to GDP (PRIVO) on the share of domestic debt in total debt appears to be positive for high income countries. This implies that the association between government debt and the size of bank loans to private sector is not necessarily negative. Yet, consistent with results obtained by Guscina (2008) and Hauner (2008) the negative coefficient on PRIVO was observed for low and medium income countries subsamples.

The results suggest that higher inflation is associated with a lower share of domestic debt in total debt only in high income countries. Whereas the inflation rate has no significant impact on domestic debt share in total debt for middle and low income countries. The regression results confirm that an unstable monetary environment characterized by high exchange rate volatility hinder the development of the domestic debt market.

In line with the notion that quality of institutions are crucial to the development of a domestic debt market, we observed the positive effect of ICRG composite risk index on domestic debt share for all subsamples. It also should be noted that the regression results on other institutional variables, such as Government stability and Law and order lends some support to the hypothesis that the issuance of domestic debt may be less relevant in stable institutional environments since the collateral or risk diversification function that a given type of debt performs on banks' balance sheets will play a smaller role once the country has stable governance committed to law and order.

Another noteworthy insight emerged is that higher savings rates do not necessarily translate into higher domestic debt share in total government debt.

The results are consistent with the idea that financial development is greater where constituency favors financial development and rejects inflation. They also support the hypothesis that, in a given group of countries a more developed banking sector offers the possibility of issuing more domestic debt. This nexus suggests the hypothesis that, with financial development, a constituency against inflation will be established. Or, the mere existence of a banking sector in a particular country supports financial development as well as anti-inflation policy. In line with this hypothesis, one could explain the tendency of countries with greater financial development to issue more domestic debt (in local currency), as there are banks holding this debt and inflation is under control.

While this paper has helped to understand the importance of financial development to create a domestic debt market, the study in the direction of causality between financial development and inflation (proxy of macroeconomic stability) merits further research. Low inflation may be necessary for financial development, which is crucial in creating a domestic debt market. But, once financial markets are developed, they may also create a pledge against inflation.

Chapter 3

PUBLIC DEBT, FINANCIAL INSTITUTIONS, AND INFLATION

ABSTRACT

This chapter explores the role of a country's financial institutions' development in reducing the inflationary-bias, to the extent that one of the channels of outstanding debt reduction available to policymakers appears to be associated with a burst in inflation or with a combination of governments' austerity plans and a steady dose of inflation. Institutional framework versus debt management is the key feature of our model of sovereign borrowing. In this model, the government has an incentive to inflate in order to reduce the burden of conventional taxation and also exploit redistribution effects of monetary policy.

Our analysis emphasizes the relevance of the financial sector development in promoting domestic versus external debt instruments and reducing the inflationary-bias. We show that, in financially less-developed and under-productive economies, when redistribution effects are unimportant, the government finds it optimal to issue inflation-indexed debt (or foreign currency debt) to reduce the inflationary-bias. Conversely, in more efficient systems (which allow banks to be more leveraged and redistribution becomes an important source of financing productive investment), the government issues domestic debt and lowers inflation in states of nature when productivity is high in order to redistribute wealth in favor of banks, thereby enhancing investment and growth. A main finding of this paper is that institutional development is crucial to the choice of denomination of public debt and to the avoidance the inflationary-bias.

3.1. INTRODUCTION

As we have shown in the previous chapter, financial sector development plays a key role in the development of the domestic bonds market which, in turn, supports the issuance of more local currency debt instruments. At the same time, financial development and domestic currency debt tend to be associated with macroeconomic stability. In effect, empirical evidence suggests that countries with an unstable macro environment and high-inflation episodes also have more foreign currency (or inflation-indexed) debt instruments than relatively more stable economies. In this paper, we address these issues and further explore the link among inflation, domestic financial markets and public debt management. We build a simple finite horizon model of public borrowing in which the government can decide to inflate part of its domestic obligations away. To the extent that the ex post real value of debt can be reduced by inflation with a discretionary monetary policy, the government has an incentive to inflate in order to reduce the burden of conventional taxation and also exploit redistribution effects of monetary policy.

The literature on the inflationary-bias problem suggests that the role of contractual arrangements, like indexation (Back and Musgrave, 1941; Lucas and Stokey, 1983; Calvo, 1988; etc.) and, conversely, the set-up of institutional arrangements, like central-bank independence (Rogoff, 1985; Alesina and Gatti, 1995; Walsh, 1995; etc.), are the ways to limit the inflationary pressures in society. Although, the importance of the intertemporal dimension of the relationship between the policymaker and the private agents has been highlighted by Barro and Gordon (1983), who suggested that building up an anti-inflationary reputation may help reduce the inflationary-bias. Diverging from the conventional literature, Chari, Kehoe and Prescott (1989), McCallum (1997) and Piga (2000) have argued, that the political approach to monetary policy provides a better account for deriving institutional solutions to this bias. Particular attention is also given to the implications of public debt (Cukierman, 1994; Beetsma and Bovenberg, 1997) and to its composition (Falcetti and Missale, 2002).

Our approach instead stresses the role of a country's financial institutions' development in reducing the government's temptation to inflate. Within our framework, the result of the existence of domestic currency debt does not depend on the government's reputation for low inflation. We believe that institutional framework versus debt management is the relevant feature of a more general model of sovereign borrowing. Furthermore, reputation problems are dealt more effectively with the strength of institutional setup. Our analysis emphasizes that countries with more developed financial institutions are likely to issue more domestic currency debt, which is coherent with stylized facts on the growing share of domestic debt in total debt across the middle and low-income countries since the 1990s.

Our approach is related to the Piga's (2000) intuition, who consider a mechanism of political models in which the origins of the inflationary-bias lie as in the institutions themselves, but also, in the structure of society itself which entails 2 constituencies, arising from bondholders (pressing for deflation) versus taxpayers (in favor of inflation), engaged in lobbying to influence the government stance on redistribution through inflation. This work argues that any level of central bank independence can be overcome by strong enough pressures for unexpected inflation arising from society. In our model biases arising from society is captured by the level of development of financial institutions (α). We show that, in financially less-developed and under-productive economies, when redistribution effects are unimportant, the government finds it optimal to issue inflation-indexed debt (or foreign currency debt) to reduce the inflationary-bias. Conversely, in more efficient systems (which allow banks to be more leveraged and redistribution becomes an important source of financing productive investment), the government issues domestic debt and lowers inflation in states of nature when productivity is high to redistribute wealth in favor of banks, thereby enhancing investment and growth. Hence, the model suggests some intuition as to why financial development, i.e. an efficient banking sector, is instrumental to the creation of a domestic bond market and why such development is associated with lower equilibrium inflation.

The modeling approach we follow owes to Gennaioli et al., (2010), who built a model wherein sovereign defaults weaken banks' balance sheets because banks hold sovereign bonds, causing private credit to decline. This paper builds on this contribution using a framework in which the government can affect the real cost of the debt with a steady inflation and redistribute in favor of banks. In our setting, we distinguish between the nominal versus foreign currency denominated public bonds, analyzing the stance of the benevolent government, whose repayment decision through surprise inflation or conventional taxation seeks to optimize the burden of costs on the domestic economy and maximize the welfare of domestic residents.

The remainder of the chapter is structured as follows. The next section presents the model. The third section analyzes the inflation constituency. The fourth section describes the equilibrium of the model. The paper concludes with the discussion of the results.

3.2. The Model

3.2.1. Setup

Our setting considers *a three-period* $(t = 0, 1, 2)$ model of a small, financially closed economy, in which the government can sell bonds to foreign and domestic residents but the latter cannot borrow or lend internationally. The following players are included in our framework: a benevolent government, savers, banks, and international financial market.

A fraction β of domestic agents consists of banks (B) and a remaining fraction $(1-\beta)$ consists of savers (S). All agents are risk neutral and indifferent to consumption in the three dates. Government bonds are the only available financial assets in period $t = 0$. An International financial market is able to lend/borrow any amount at an expected return equal to the interest rate r_t^*. At the beginning of the period $t = 0$, all domestic residents receive an endowment equal to $\omega_0 < 1$. Savers deposit their endowment in banks or invest in government bonds. Banks collect deposits and invest them and their endowment in government bonds.

At $t = 0$, the government wants to undertake an indivisible public project of size 1. Given that $\omega_0 < 1$, the government also finances investment by borrowing abroad. More specifically, the government can issue one-year bonds of two types: 1) domestic debt held by domestic residents, denominated in domestic (nominal) and/or foreign currency (indexed), and 2) external foreign currency debt held by foreign residents. Domestic nominal bonds are subject to inflation risk at $t = 1$. That is, the government opportunistically decides which fraction of its maturing obligations to repay in real terms at $t = 1$ and chooses how much to devalue by inflating, i.e. chooses π on a discretionary basis (by using monetary policy). If the government doesn't inflate, it must raise conventional taxes.

By using inflation to reduce the face value of debt, the government bears an inflation cost but there is no change in total welfare, W. Alternatively, conventional taxation causes a deadweight loss of $W(1-\varepsilon)$ which is assumed to be linear in taxes, T. Since the government is benevolent, its repayment decision seeks to optimize the burden of costs on the domestic economy and maximize the welfare of domestic residents.

At the beginning of the period $t = 1$, each domestic resident again receives $\omega_{1j} > 1$, for $j \in \{S, B\}$. We use $\omega_1 = \beta\omega_{1b} + (1-\beta)\omega_{1S} > 1$ to denote the total endowment of the domestic economy at $t = 1$.

At the beginning of this period domestic Banks have access to a linear investment project in the economy's productive sector. This project yields A_j units of the consumption good at $t = 2$ per unit invested at $t = 1$. Productivity is a stochastic variable and becomes known at the beginning of $t = 1$, taking value A_H with probability p and A_L with probability $(1-p)$. Bankers need to borrow to finance this investment.

We refer to claims issued by the government as public bonds (b) and to claims issued by banks as deposits (d). We use b_j and d_{jt} to respectively denote the holdings by agents of type $j \in \{S, B\}$ of public bonds and of deposits originated at time $t \in \{0,1\}$. Bank deposits are only in domestic currency. r_b and r_b^* stand for the contractual nominal interest rates promised by nominal domestic and external public bonds respectively, and r_{dt} stands for the contractual interest rate promised by deposits originated at t. The expected real return on all assets is the same and equal to r^*, i.e. $\mathbb{E}[r_b - \gamma\pi] = = \mathbb{E}[r_d - \gamma\pi] = r^*$.

We assume that the income of domestic residents is taxed at a uniform rate, while nonresident's income is not taxed.

Private deposits are subject to imperfect court enforcement: if a bank defaults, only a share α of its revenues is seizeable by depositors. If α=1, the bank can pledge all of its revenues to depositors and financial frictions are non-existent. These frictions rise as α falls below 1. Thus, the level of α captures the level of financial development and, in particular, the strength of investor protection at home.

The relevant feature of the setup developed in this paper is that the government's repayment decision affects financial markets and investment. Otherwise stated, under the enforcement frictions, the payments (in real terms) delivered by nominal public bonds and deposits issued at $t = 0$ are ex-post contingent on the government decision to inflate which, in turn, depends on the state of productivity $\psi = \{H, L\}$ realized at $t = 1$[1].

---

[1] In the specification of the present model, repudiation has no reputation effects. That is, there is, by construction, no possibility of future sanctions after repudiation.

The timing of events is as follows:

- Stage $t = 0$: The domestic residents receive per capita endowment equal to $\omega_0 < 1$. The government looks for loanable funds from its own citizens as well as from international investors and makes known the composition of debt to be issued, specifying the share of (one-period) nominal bonds, b and the residual share of (one-period) foreign currency denominated bonds, b^*. Given the respective contractual interest rates r_b, r_d and r^* on domestic government bonds, deposits and foreign bonds, agents make investment/borrowing decisions and optimally determine their portfolios.
- Stage $t = 1$: The state of productivity $\psi = \{H, L\}$ is revealed. Domestic residents receive ω_{1j}, $j \epsilon \{B, S\}$. All assets issued at $t = 0$ mature. The government decides whether to repay its outstanding obligations $[(1 + r_b)b + (1 + r_{b*})b^*]$, where $(b + b^*)$ denotes the total amount of bonds issued by the government. There is a trade-off between inflation, π and conventional taxation. More precisely, since only the nominal debt is sensitive to the inflation tax, the government chooses what share of its outstanding nominal obligations $(1 + r_b - - \gamma\pi)b$ to repay via taxation. We assume that the income of domestic residents (bankers and savers) is taxed at a uniform rate, while nonresident's income is not taxed. The welfare loss will be higher if only conventional taxes are used. As a result, a higher rate of inflation, π is associated with lower taxation of domestic residents[2]. At the beginning of this period Bankers borrow from savers to invest in the productive technology.
- Stage $t = 2$: returns at $t = 1$ are realized and consumption takes place.

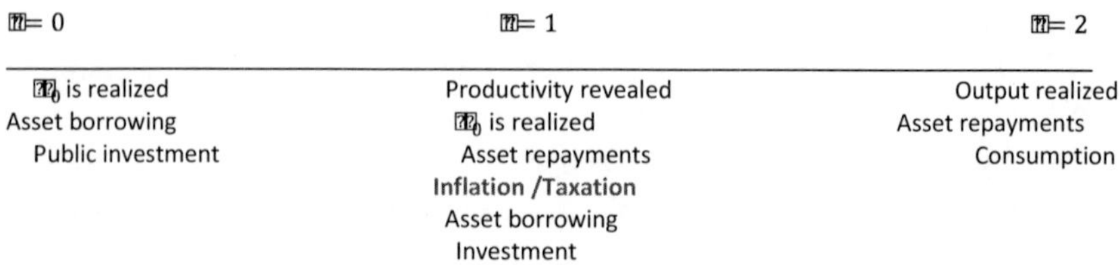

Figure 1.

[2] On average $r=r^*+\mathbb{E}\pi$ and $\mathbb{E}T$=const, but π and T are different across states of productivity.

To model these players, we derive their objective functions by specifying their preferences as follows.

a. Domestic Agents

Each agent seeks to maximize his utility:

$$\text{Max } c_1 + \delta c_2$$

$$\{d_0, b_0^*, b_0, d_1\}$$

subject to $c_2 \leq \omega_1 + (1 + r^*)b_j^* + (1 + r_b - \gamma\pi)b_j + (1 + r_d - \gamma\pi)d_{j0} - T$

$c_2 \geq 0$

where, $\delta\epsilon(0,1)$ is the discount factor and T denotes taxes paid by domestic residents. The utility function is linear with a discount factor $\delta = (1 + r^*)^{-1}$, while the income of domestic residents is taxed at a uniform rate. We assume perfect substitutability and $A_j \geq 1 + r^*$ imply that all consumption is in period $t = 2$.

Savers

In period $t = 0$, each Saver decides the fraction of its savings and public bondholdings $\{d_0, b_0\}$ to be deposited in the banks or invested in public bonds, taking endowment ω_0 as given. Banks deposits yield a return of $(1 + + r_d - \gamma\pi)d_{b0}$, foreign currency public bonds yield a return of $(1 + r^*)b_s^*$, while domestic currency public bonds yield a return of $(1 + r_b - \gamma\pi)b_s$ in the subsequent period. If the interest rate on deposits, r_d, equals that on domestic bonds, r_b, savers are indifferent to the choice between holding domestic public bonds and bank deposits.

The impact of government inflation, π, in $t = 1$ on savers wealth depends on their holdings of nominal assets. If the share of nominal assets they own exceeds their share of the tax burden, T, required to service the debt, their wealth decreases in π. Thus, for this agent, the cost of inflation is larger than its benefits. The opposite is true when the share of nominal assets agents own is less than their share of the tax burden required to service the debt.

Banks

Banks compete for savings of the consumers in period $t = 0$. We assume that the deposits are merely in domestic currency. The government bonds are the only available financial assets to banks by this period (i.e. banks do not hold deposits of other banks). Banks choose their holdings of public bonds in order to transfer resources between periods. Since public bonds (domestic and external) also must be attractive to the international financial market, their expected return must satisfy: $\mathbb{E}[r_b - \gamma\pi] \geq r^*$[3]. Furthermore, bankers, who are risk neutral, require the same real expected return on nominal and foreign currency denominated public bonds. Thus, the real interest rate on domestic public bonds should be defined implicitly:

$$p(1 + r_b - \gamma\pi^H) + (1 - p)(1 + r_b - \gamma\pi^L) = 1 + r^* \quad (1)$$

where p is the probability of the high productivity state.

Let W_{b1} be the wealth (net of taxes) of the bank at the end of $t = 1$; this includes the bank's endowment ω_{b1} plus any payments obtained from bonds purchased at $t = 0$ less payments made on deposits issued at $t = 0$. Upon learning the state of productivity $\{H, L\}$ at $t = 1$, a bank entering the period chooses its level of deposits d_{b1} by solving:

$$\underset{d_{b1}}{Max}\; A_\psi(-d_{b1} + W_{b1}) + (1 + r_{d1})d_{b1} \text{ subject to,} \quad (2^1)$$

$$-d_{b1}(1 + r_{d1}) \leq \alpha A_\psi(d_{b1} + W_{b1}) \text{ for } d_{b1} < 0, \quad (2^2)$$

for any given level of productivity $\psi = \{H, L\}$, where equation (2^1) represents the bank's credit constraint. The equilibrium interest rate on deposits must be lower than the productivity of investment, i.e. $1 + r_{d1} \leq A_H$. This enables banks to earn rents from investment equal to $A_H - (1 + r_{d1})$. Otherwise, banks would not want to attract any deposits. It must also be true that $1 + + r_{d1} > \alpha A_H$. Otherwise, a bank could attract an infinite amount of deposits. Subject to these credit constraints the banking system's demand of funds at $t = 1$ in the high productivity state is given by

$$D = \beta \frac{\alpha A_H}{(1 + r_{d1}) - \alpha A_H} W_b \quad (3^1)$$

while, aggregate investment by the banking system is given by

[3] For simplicity, there is no segmentation between the domestic and foreign bond market.

$$I = \beta \frac{1+r_{d1}}{(1+r_{d1})-\alpha A_H} W_b \tag{3^2}$$

Equations (3^1) and (3^2) illustrate that a higher level of α, i.e. a higher level of financial development, enables banks to increase their leverage, attracting more deposits, to expand investment in the economy's productive sector at $t = 1$. The social surplus yielded by this investment equals

$$\frac{A_H - (1+r^*)}{(1+r^*) - \alpha A_H} \beta W_b \tag{3^3}$$

While, in the low productivity states it holds: $A_L = 1 + r^*$.

It should be noted that the real wealth of banks, as well as the need for intermediation at $t = 1$, depends on the equilibrium portfolios at $t = 0$ and on the impact of the government's repayment decision.

This is because inflation triggers a deterioration in banks' asset position to the extent that the share of nominal bonds in total debtholding of banks' is greater than deposits. Furthermore, the government's decision to inflate results in fewer resources in the banking system, which in turn restricts lending to the domestic productive sector. By redistributing wealth away from banks, inflation may ultimately reduce investment and output.

b. The Government

The government is benevolent. Its optimal decision balances the cost of inflation against its benefits to maximize consumption in the final period. The objective function for the government is the following:

$$Max\ C = Y - \frac{1}{2}\mu\pi^2 - \lambda T \tag{4}$$

where π is the inflation chosen by the government in stage $t = 1$ of the game and Y is the total output of the economy in period $t = 2$, i.e. the sum of total domestic wealth (the first term in brackets below) plus the social surplus generated by productive sector investment in the high productivity state:

$$Y^H = [\beta W_b + (1-\beta)W_s] + \frac{A_H - (1+r^*)}{(1+r^*) - \alpha A_H} \beta W_b \tag{5^1}$$

While, in low productivity state, Y is defined as:

$$Y^L = \beta W_b + (1 - \beta) W_s \tag{5^2}$$

In period $t = 0$, the government must choose the optimal composition of public debt: b - the share of nominal debt and b^* - the residual share of foreign currency debt. At the end of period $t = 1$, the government observes the productivity $\{H, L\}$ and then makes a decision to inflate. In particular, the government chooses the appropriate level of inflation π with the goal of maximizing social welfare. The real value of the debt is determined by its composition and the impact of unexpected inflation. By inflating, the government can only affect the nominal debt (insofar as monetary policy does not systematically affect the real exchange rate[4]). To understand the government's incentives, note that debt repayment affects the domestic distribution of wealth. The wealth of an agent of type $j \epsilon \{B, S\}$ at t=1 is given by

$$W_j \leq \omega_{1j} + (1 + r^*) b_j^* + (1 + r_b - \gamma\pi) b_j + (1 + r_d - \gamma\pi) d_{j0} - T \tag{6^1}$$

Where $T = (1 + r^*) b^* + (1 + r_b - \gamma\pi) b$ (6²)
$d_{jt} < 0$ for banks

Equation (6¹) shows that the impact of government inflation decision $(1 + + r_b - \gamma\pi) b_j$ on the wealth of type - j individuals depends on their bondholdings: the wealth of these individuals is increasing in the rate of inflation if the share of the nominal assets, b_j and d_j, they own is lower than their share of the tax burden, T, required to service the debt. Thus, for this type of agent, the cost of conventional tax repayment is larger than the cost of inflation. The opposite is true when the share of nominal assets, b_j and d_j, the agents own is greater than their share of the tax burden, T, required to service the debt.

3.2.2. Benchmark Cases

We examine two different cases. In the first specification, we consider a case, in which the banks hold only domestic nominal debt. This enables us to

[4] Obviously, this is the case if PPP holds. In that case the value of foreign currency debt would depend on unexpected foreign inflation.

shed light on the mechanisms operating in our model. In the second case, we extend the initial specification and let the banks hold nominal as well as foreign currency debt: ϕ represents the share of nominal bonds, and $(1-\phi)$ represents the residual share of foreign currency bonds in total domestic bank debtholding. In equilibrium, ϕ depends upon the government choice for the composition of public debt. We maintain the assumption that deposits are merely in domestic currency.

3.3. Inflation Constituency

In this section, we discuss the motivation behind the government's choice to inflate away its maturing domestic obligations.

The government's trade-off is straightforward. On the one hand, domestic residents (taxpayers) are interested in reducing the real value of public debt through unexpected inflation to reduce their real tax burden. In our model, foreign currency debt is not sensitive to the inflation tax. Inflation can only have an impact on all holders of nominal debt by an equal fashion. To visualize the exposure of the domestic economy to nominal public debt, we define b_d as the nominal debt purchased by domestic residents, b_f as the nominal debt that is purchased by foreign creditors, while b* stands for the foreign currency debt. Assuming that the public debt should be repaid at $t=1$ and using a linear approximation for the impact of inflation, the tax rate, T, imposed on domestic residents in order to make repayments on public debt is equal to:

$$T=(1+r^{*})b^{*}+(1+r_{b}-\gamma\pi)(b_{d}+b_{f}) \tag{7}$$

If foreigners hold some nominal debt, inflating the debt lowers the real value of the debt to be repaid and increases the total wealth (net of taxes) of domestic agents by reducing tax repayments abroad, i.e. it increases the first term in equation (5^1). Intuitively, the higher the ratio of nominal debt held by foreigners, the higher the marginal benefit of inflation, since a unit increase in the level of inflation corresponds to a larger absolute reduction in debt repayments. On the other hand, if banks hold a sufficiently large amount of nominal government bonds (larger than deposits), inflation negatively affects the asset position of the banks. As inflation hurts the net wealth of the banking system (the second term of equation (5^1)), productive investment falls. This investment cost is increasing in the rate of inflation. By redistributing wealth away from banks, inflation may ultimately reduce the level of output. Inflation redistribution effects turn out to be costly if investment is productive. Therefore, the government's incentive to inflate is higher in the low productive state ($A_b = A_L = 1 + r^*$) when the marginal output cost of inflation is lower.

To further reveal government's incentive to inflate its way out of debt and explore the exposure mechanism of domestic economy to public debt, let's suppose that all domestic wealth is invested in nominal public bonds, while foreign investors hold foreign currency debt. In this case, no redistribution takes place and the government has a strong incentive to inflate the economy for all realizations of the state of productivity at $t = 1$. Consequently, the economy bears only the cost of inflation.

The other extreme case appears when all agents hold only foreign currency debt. As this eliminates the incentive for the government to inflate, inflation would be equal to $\pi = 0$. We shall show that, in general, this is not optimal, as the government has a preference to have $\mathbb{E}\pi$ higher on average and the possibility to exploit distributional effects of monetary policy. The crucial point of redistribution stays on the level of nominal assets (debtholding, b_b, and deposits, d_{b0}). In turn, the higher the part of the wealth invested in foreign currency debt the lower is π. The observed extreme cases point out that the government's debt issuance decision at t=0 affects inflation decisions at t=1.

Since, other things being equal, the motivation of the government to inflate is stronger the higher is the share of nominal debt held by foreigners, below we explore the cases when foreigners only hold the foreign currency (inflation-indexed) debt. We denote by $\alpha^{max}(\beta)$ the level of investor protection beyond which in high productive state all domestic wealth is invested. In this case α also captures the strength of financial development.

3.4. Equilibrium

An equilibrium of our economy assumes rationality in terms of the portfolio decisions by agents, a government repayment decision and a set of expected and ex-post returns on assets, such that (i) asset markets clear; (ii) returns on government bonds are consistent with government optimization, and (iii) returns on deposits are consistent with imperfect enforcement.

There are two types of equilibria analyzed: In the first specification, we consider a case, in which the banks hold only nominal debt. The second specification expands the analysis to the more general case by allowing nominal debtholdings by banks, ϕ_b, to vary with ϕ - the share of nominal debt in total debtholdings of banks. We start with the equilibrium in deposit markets at $t = 1$, after that working our way back to study the market at $t = 0$. The proofs of the results are presented in Appendix VI.

3.4.1. Deposit Markets

a. Deposit Market at t=1

Since the banks enter the period $t = 1$ with holdings of nominal government bonds, the government's decision to inflate part of its nominal domestic obligations affects the asset position of the banks. The wealth of banks after the government decision to inflate would be:

$$W_{1b} = \omega_{1b} + (1 + r_b - \gamma\pi)b_b - (1 + r_d - \gamma\pi)\frac{1-\beta}{\beta}d_{b0} - T \quad (8)$$

where $T = \beta(1 + r_b - \gamma\pi)b_b + (1 - \beta)(1 + r^*)b_s^* + (1 + r^*)b_f^*$ (9)

Banks invest these resources in the productive sector at the end of period $t = 1$. Hence, investment by a bank is equal to:

$$I = \omega_{1b} + (1 + r_b - \gamma\pi)b_b - (1 + r_d - \gamma\pi)\frac{1-\beta}{\beta}d_{b0} - T \quad (10)$$

Consequently, investments in the production sector are less than or equal to the total banks' wealth (net of taxes) at $t = 1$, while aggregate investment by the banking system is defined by equation (3^2):

$$I = \beta\frac{1+r_{d1}}{(1+r_{d1})-\alpha A_H}W_b.$$

Hence, investment in the economy's productive sector at $t = 1$ increases with real wealth of the banking system and, also, with a higher level of financial development (through the term α), which allows banks to increase their leverage, thereby attracting more deposits to expand investment.

b. Deposit Market at t=0

In period $t = 0$ banks can only invest in government bonds. We assume that they offer deposits only in domestic currency. In the first specification, we consider a case, in which the banks hold only nominal debt. After that, we extend the initial specification and let the banks to hold as a share ϕ of nominal debt as well as foreign currency debt $(1-\phi)$. The nominal interest rates on domestic public bonds satisfies

$$p(1+r_b-\gamma\pi^H)+(1-p)(1+r_b-\gamma\pi^L)=1+r^*$$

According to this equation, the nominal interest rate on domestic public bonds, r_b, is defined implicitly. If the nominal interest rate on deposits, r_d, equals the interest rate on domestic bonds, r_b, savers are indifferent between holding domestic public bonds and bank deposits. We assume that, in the event of such indifference, they choose to deposit part of their initial endowment in banks and invest the rest of their endowment in foreign currency bonds. This case arises for sufficiently low α. Consequently, total deposits raised by banks at $t = 0$ to purchase the public bonds are given by: $d_{total} = (1-\beta)(\omega_0 - b_s^*)$, while deposits raised by 1 bank are expressed as: $d_{1bank} = \frac{(1-\beta)}{\beta}(\omega_0 - b_s^*)$. Due to enforcement frictions, expected payments on deposits cannot exceed a share α of the bank's expected revenues at $t = 1$. Thus, any such bank can raise an amount of deposits equal to:

$$(1+r_d-\gamma\pi)\cdot\frac{(1-\beta)}{\beta}(\omega_0-b_s^*)\le\alpha(\omega_{1b}+(1+r_b-\gamma\pi)b_b) \qquad (11)$$

If the amount of foreign currency bonds, b_s^*, is held by savers, a bank's holding of nominal bonds is equal to: $b_b = \omega_0 + \frac{(1-\beta)}{\beta}(\omega_0 - b_s^*)$. This case arises if $\alpha \le \alpha_0(\beta)$. When instead $\alpha > \alpha_0(\beta)$, savers deposit their whole endowment in banks and all domestic endowments are used by banks to purchase public bonds : $b_b = \frac{\omega_0}{\beta}$.

3.4.2. The Composition of Public Debt versus Inflation

a. First Specification

In this specification, we consider a case, in which the banks hold only nominal domestic debt. Applying definition (8) and (9), the wealth of banks (net of taxes) in $t = 1$ is given by

$$W_{1b} = \omega_{1b} + (1-\beta)b_s^*(r - r^* - \gamma\pi) - (1 + r^*)\mathrm{b}_\mathrm{f}^* \quad (12)$$

This equation makes clear that the bank's wealth is decreasing in π. Note that unexpected inflation increases saver's wealth (net of taxes) at $t = 1$:

$$W_{1s} = \omega_{1b} - \beta b_s^*(r - r^* - \gamma\pi) - (1 + r^*)\mathrm{b}_\mathrm{f}^* \quad (13)$$

By applying the definition of Y from equation (5^1) and (5^2), we get

$$Y^\psi = W_1 + \frac{A_H - (1+r^*)}{(1+r^*) - \alpha A_H}\beta\left[\omega_{1b} + (1-\beta)\mathrm{b}_\mathrm{s}^*\left(r - r^* - \gamma\pi^\psi\right) - \right.$$
$$\left. - (1 + r^*)\mathrm{b}_\mathrm{f}^*\right] - (1 + \mathrm{r}^*)\mathrm{b}_\mathrm{f}^* \quad (14)$$

The government is benevolent and maximizes the welfare function (4) with respect to π:

$$\max_\pi C = Y - \frac{1}{2}\mu\pi^2 - \lambda T$$

subject to

$$c_2 \leq \omega_1 + (1 + r^*)\mathrm{b}_\mathrm{j}^* + (1 + r_b - \gamma\pi)b_j + (1 + r_d - \gamma\pi)d_{j0} - T$$
$$c_2 \geq 0$$

where Y and T is defined from (14) and (9) respectively. Replacing them in the objective function, the government's first-order condition with respect to π yields

$$-\frac{A_H - (1+r^*)}{(1+r^*) - \alpha A_H}\beta(1-\beta)b_s^*\gamma - \mu\pi^\psi + \lambda\beta\gamma[\omega_0 + \frac{(1-\beta)}{\beta}(\omega_0 - b_s^*)] \geq 0 \quad (15)$$

It is straightforward to prove that equilibrium inflation, respectively for the low and high states of productivity, yields

$$\pi^L = \frac{1}{\mu}\lambda\gamma[\omega_0 - (1-\beta)b_s^*] \tag{16}$$

$$\pi^H = \frac{1}{\mu}\lambda\gamma[\omega_0 - (1-\beta)b_s^*] - \frac{1}{\mu}\frac{A_H - (1+r^*)}{(1+r^*) - \alpha A_H}\beta(1-\beta)b_s^*\gamma = \pi^L - $$
$$- \frac{1}{\mu}\frac{A_H - (1+r^*)}{(1+r^*) - \alpha A_H}\beta(1-\beta)b_s^*\gamma \tag{17}$$

While, the nominal interest rate on domestic public bonds, defined implicitly, equals

$$r = r^* + \frac{\lambda}{\mu}\gamma^2[\omega_0 - (1-\beta)b_s^*)] - \frac{P}{\mu}\frac{A_H - (1+r^*)}{(1+r^*) - \alpha A_H}\beta(1-\beta)b_s^*\gamma^2 \tag{18}$$

By comparing (16) and (17), inflation in the high productive state is lower than in the low productive state. After a state of high productivity is revealed, the decision to inflate results in a reduction in investment and output. If the government decides not to inflate, it only does so when productivity is high, i.e. when $A_H > 1 + r^*$, implying that in such state the government must pay an interest rate

$$r - p\gamma\pi^H = r^* + (1-p)\gamma\pi^L.$$

Expected total output of the economy can be expressed as

$$\mathbb{E}Y = pY^H + (1-p)Y^L$$

where, the total output Y^H of the domestic economy in the high productivity state can be written as

$$Y^H = W_1 + \frac{A_H - (1+r^*)}{(1+r^*) - \alpha A_H}\beta[\omega_{1b} + (1-\beta)\mathrm{b}_\mathrm{s}^*(r - r^* - \gamma\pi^H) - $$
$$- (1+r^*)\mathrm{b}_\mathrm{f}^*] - (1+\mathrm{r}^*)\mathrm{b}_\mathrm{f}^* \tag{19}$$

Hence, total output in the high productivity state equals the total domestic wealth at t=1 plus the surplus generated by investment in the economy's productive sector.

More precisely, the second term captures the impact of government's decision to inflate on investment. While, total output in low productivity state describes the decline in total domestic wealth caused by repayment and can be written as

$$Y^L = W_1 - (1 + r^*)b_f^* \tag{20}$$

For simplicity, define as ϑ the surplus generated by the productive sector investment

$$\vartheta = \frac{A_H - (1+r^*)}{(1+r^*) - \alpha A_H} \tag{21}$$

Then, using the expressions for π from equation (17), for r from equation (18) and for Y^H and Y^L from equations (19) and (20) respectively, we can define expected total output of the economy as

$$\mathbb{E}Y = pY^H + (1-p)Y^L = W_1 - (1+r^*)b_f^*(1 + p\vartheta\beta) + p\vartheta\beta\omega_{1b} + \\ + \underbrace{\frac{\gamma^2 p(1-p)\beta^2\Theta^2(1-\beta)^2 b_s^{*2}}{\mu}}_{Gain\ from\ having\ nominal\ debt} \tag{22}$$

Solving the optimization problem for the expected consumption, call it $\mathbb{E}c^D$ - if the government issues only nominal domestic debt and $\mathbb{E}c^F$ - if government issue only foreign currency debt, yields

$$\mathbb{E}c^D = \mathbb{E}Y^D - \frac{\mu}{2}\mathbb{E}\pi^2 - \lambda\overline{\mathbb{E}T}$$

and

$$\mathbb{E}c^F = \mathbb{E}Y^F - 0 - \lambda\overline{\mathbb{E}T}$$

where, $\mathbb{E}Y^F = W_1 - (1+r^*)b_f^*(1 + p\vartheta\beta) + p\vartheta\beta\omega_{1b}$
and

$$\mathbb{E}\pi = p\pi^H + (1-p)\pi^L = \frac{\gamma}{\mu}\lambda[\omega_0 - (1-\beta)b_s^*] - p\frac{\gamma}{\mu}\,\vartheta\beta(1-\beta)b_s^*,$$

hence depends from λ.

The difference between $\mathbb{E}c^D$ and $\mathbb{E}c^F$ suggests that there is a tradeoff between the burden of inflation cost on the domestic economy and government's gain from having nominal domestic debt:

$$\mathbb{E}c^D - \mathbb{E}c^F = \mathbb{E}Y^D - \mathbb{E}Y^F - \frac{\mu}{2}\mathbb{E}\pi^2 = \underbrace{\frac{\gamma^2 p(1-p)\beta^2\theta^2(1-\beta)^2 b_s^{*2}}{\mu}}_{Gain\ from\ nominal\ debt} - \underbrace{-\frac{\mu}{2}\mathbb{E}\pi^2}_{Loss\ from\ nominal\ debt} \quad (23)$$

Hence, the more nominal contracts there are in this economy, the higher the inflationary-bias.

b. Second Specification

In this section, we focus on the more general case where the banks hold as nominal as well as foreign currency debt: ϕ stands for the share of nominal bonds and $(1-\phi)$ the residual share of foreign currency bonds in total bank debtholding. The maximization problem of the consumers remains unchanged. Under this setting, taxes paid by domestic residents are equal to the following

$$T = \phi\beta(1+r-\gamma\pi)b_b + (1-\phi)\beta(1+r^*)b_b + (1-\beta)(1+r^*)b_s^* + + (1+r^*)b_f^* \quad (24)$$

As expected, the wealth of banks (net of taxes) is decreasing in unexpected inflation:

$$W_{1b} = \omega_{1b} + (r - r^* - \gamma\pi)\frac{(1-\beta)}{\beta}[\underbrace{\phi(\omega_0 - (1-\beta)b_s^*)}_{nominal\ bonds} - \underbrace{(\omega_0 - b_s^*)}_{deposits\ in\ domestic\ currency}] - -(1+r^*)b_f^* \quad (25)$$

While, the Saver's wealth (net of taxes) is increasing in π proportionally to the level of the nominal debt held by banks and at $t = 1$ could be expressed as

$$W_{1s} = \omega_{1s} - (r - r^* - \gamma\pi)[\underbrace{\phi(\omega_0 - (1-\beta)b_s^*)}_{Nominal\ bonds\ of\ banks} - \underbrace{(\omega_0 - b_s^*)}_{deposits\ in\ domestic\ currency}] - -(1+r^*)b_f^* \quad (26)$$

Note that there are no aggregate effects from inflation as

$$\beta W_{1b} + (1-\beta)W_{1s} = \beta\omega_{1b} + (1-\beta)\omega_{1s} - (1+r^*)b_f^* = W_1 - (1+r^*)b_f^*$$

By using the definition of total output from equation (5^1) and (5^2) in high and low productivity states respectively, we get:

$$Y^H = W_1 + \vartheta\beta\omega_{1b} + (r - r^* - \gamma\pi)\vartheta(1-\beta)[\phi(\omega_0 - (1-\beta)\mathrm{b}_\mathrm{s}^*) - -(\omega_0 - \mathrm{b}_\mathrm{s}^*)] - \vartheta(1+r^*)\beta\mathrm{b}_\mathrm{f}^* - (1+r^*)b_f^* \quad (27^1)$$

where $\vartheta = \frac{A_H - (1+r^*)}{(1+r^*) - \alpha A_H}$, and

$$Y^L = \beta W_{1b} + (1-\beta)W_{1s} = W_1 - (1+r^*)b_f^* \quad (27^2)$$

Expected output can be expressed in the form of:

$\mathbb{E}Y = pY^H + (1-p)Y^L$, and will be:

$$\mathbb{E}Y = W_1 + p[\vartheta\beta\omega_{1b} + (r - r^* - \gamma\pi^H)\vartheta(1 - -\beta)[\phi(\omega_0 - (1-\beta)b_s^*) - (\omega_0 - b_s^*)] - \vartheta(1+r^*)\beta b_f^*] - (1+r^*)b_f^* \quad (28)$$

The government is benevolent and maximizes the same welfare function (4) with respect to π:

$$\max_{\pi} C = Y - \frac{1}{2}\mu\pi^2 - \lambda T$$

The first-order condition, $\frac{\partial C}{\partial \pi}=0$, implies that the equilibrium inflation, in low and high productivity states respectively, satisfies the following conditions

$$\pi^L = \frac{\gamma}{\mu}\lambda\phi[\omega_0 - (1-\beta)b_s^*] \quad (29^1)$$

and

$$\pi^H = \frac{\gamma}{\mu}\lambda\phi[\omega_0 - (1-\beta)b_s^*] - - \frac{\gamma}{\mu}\vartheta(1-\beta)[\phi[\omega_0 - (1-\beta)b_s^*] - (\omega_0 - b_s^*)] = = \pi^L - \frac{\gamma}{\mu}\vartheta(1-\beta)[\phi[\omega_0 - (1-\beta)b_s^*] - (\omega_0 - b_s^*)] \quad (29^2)$$

Hence, the Inflation in low productive state is as in the first specification, except lower if $\phi<1$.

It can be shown that the nominal interest rate on domestic public bonds, defined implicitly, is equal to

$$r = r^* + \frac{\gamma^2}{\mu}\phi\lambda[\omega_0 - (1-\beta)b_s^*] - \gamma^2\frac{p}{\mu}\vartheta(1-\beta)[\phi[\omega_0 - (1-\beta)b_s^*] - -(\omega_0 - b_s^*)] \tag{30}$$

Using the expressions for π^H from equation (29[2]), for r from equation (30) and the equation (28), the expected output would be expressed in the form of

$$\mathbb{E}Y = W_1 + p\theta\beta\omega_{1b} + p(1-p)\frac{\gamma^2}{\mu}\vartheta^2(1-\beta)^2[\phi(\omega_0 - (1-\beta)b_s^*) - - (\omega_0 - b_s^*)]^2 - p\vartheta(1+r^*)\beta b_f^* - (1+r^*)b_f^*$$

We can define the optimal level of ϕ which maximizes welfare of domestic residents by deriving the maximization problem of consumption with respect to ϕ. More precisely, we look for the solution of the government's optimization problem with respect of the share of nominal debtholdings, ϕ of banks, which takes the form

$$\max_{\varphi} \mathbb{E}C = \mathbb{E}Y - \frac{1}{2}\mu\mathbb{E}\pi^2 - \lambda\mathbb{E}T \tag{31}$$

By deriving the total output of the domestic economy, with respect to ϕ, yields

$$\frac{\partial \mathbb{E}Y}{\partial \phi} = 2p(1-p)\frac{\gamma^2}{\mu}\vartheta^2(1-\beta)^2[\phi(\omega_0 - (1-\beta)b_s^*) - (\omega_0 - -b_s^*)][(\omega_0 - (1-\beta)b_s^*)] \tag{32^1}$$

where, $\omega_0 - (1-\beta)b_s^* = \beta b_b > 0$ defines total bonds held by banks.

In case $\phi(\omega_0 - (1-\beta)b_s^*) < \omega_0 - b_s^*$, i.e. for $\phi \to 0$ (the amount of nominal bonds are small), the sign of the derivative in (32[1]) indicates that inflation favors the banks and total output of the economy, $\mathbb{E}Y$ decreases with ϕ.

In case $\phi(\omega_0 - (1-\beta)b_s^*) > \omega_0 - b_s^*$, i.e. nominal bonds are greater than deposits, an increase in ϕ, also increases total output of the economy, $\mathbb{E}Y$.

By deriving the term of expected inflation (second term in (31)), with respect of ϕ, yields

$$\frac{\partial}{\partial \phi}(\frac{1}{2}\mu\mathbb{E}\pi^2) = \frac{\gamma^2}{\mu}p\beta b_b\{\lambda - \vartheta(1-\beta)\}\{\phi\lambda\beta b_b - \vartheta(1-\beta)[\phi\beta b_b - -(\omega_0 - b_s^*)]\} + (1-p)\frac{\gamma^2}{\mu}\phi\lambda^2\beta^2 b_b^2 \tag{32^2}$$

While, by deriving the term of expected taxes (third term in (31)), with respect of π, yields

$$\lambda \frac{\partial \mathbb{E}\mathrm{T}}{\partial \phi} = 0 \qquad (32^3)$$

Finally, the first-order condition of the government optimization problem with respect of φ, results

$$\frac{\partial \mathbb{E}C}{\partial \phi} = \underbrace{2p(1-p)\vartheta^2(1-\beta)^2[\phi\beta b_b - (\omega_0 - b_s^*)]}_{\textit{Distribution effect}} - p\{\lambda -$$

$$-\vartheta(1-\beta\}\{\underbrace{\phi\lambda\beta b_b}_{\pi^L \textit{ effect}} -$$

$$-\underbrace{\vartheta(1-\beta)[\phi\beta b_b - (\omega_0 - b_s^*)]\}}_{\pi^H \textit{ effect}} - (1-p)\phi\lambda^2\beta b_b \qquad (33^1)$$

We can rewrite equation (33^1) as a combination of (d, K, λ), such that

$$d = \omega_0 - b_s^*$$

$$K = \vartheta(1-\beta)$$

and λ is a marginal cost of taxation. As a result, (33^1) takes the form:

$$\frac{\partial \mathbb{E}C}{\partial \phi} = [(1-2p)pK^2 + 2pK\lambda - \lambda^2]\phi\beta b_b - [(1-2p)K + \lambda]pKd \qquad (33^2)$$

There are different cases to consider that can impact the equilibrium. A detailed derivation of these cases and proofs are relegated to Appendix VI. We summarize below our key predictions for the level of ϕ in the following preposition:

Proposition For any level of λ, there exists a level of α^* such that $\phi = 1$ whenever $\alpha > \alpha^*$, while $\phi = 0$ whenever $\alpha < \alpha^*$.

For detailed Proof See Appendix VI.

Proof Sketch: Notice that K is an increasing function of α and A_H. In the case of high probability $(p > \frac{1}{2})$ of the high productivity state, the smallest value of the marginal cost of taxation, λ, defined as: $\lambda < (2p - 1)K$, is related to the highest share of nominal domestic debt in total banks' debtholding, $\phi = 1$.

Indeed, a given level of inflation reduces λ, the greater is ϕ. Conversely, the highest value of λ, defined as: $\lambda > K[p + \sqrt{p(1-p)}]$ is related to the case when domestic banks hold only foreign currency debt, $\phi = 0$.

We have also evaluated the case when λ takes the intermediate value, defined as:

$(2p - 1)K < \lambda < K[p + \sqrt{p(1-p)}]$. Specifically, we calculated the difference between expected consumptions in two extreme cases: with the highest share of nominal domestic debt, $\phi = 1$ and with the lowest share of nominal domestic debt, $\phi = 0$ in total bondholdings of banks. Our results imply that the difference, $\mathbb{E}C_{\phi=1} - \mathbb{E}C_{\phi=0}$, between expected consumptions in two extreme cases is:

a) positive $(i.e. \mathbb{E}C_{\phi=1} - \mathbb{E}C_{\phi=0} > 0)$, once the marginal cost of taxation, λ, is close to the lower bound: $\lambda \approx (2p - 1)K$, i.e. the consumption in the case of $\phi = 1$ is higher than the consumption in the case of $\phi = 0$, and;
b) negative $(\mathbb{E}C_{\phi=1} - \mathbb{E}C_{\phi=0} < 0)$, whenever λ is close to upper bound: $\lambda \approx K[p + \sqrt{p(1-p)}]$, i.e. the consumption in the case of $\phi = 0$ is higher than the consumption in the case of $\phi = 1$.

Consequently, there are threshold levels of λ and K for which having the highest share of nominal domestic debt in total banks debtholding, $\phi = 1$ is optimal. More precisely, once $\lambda \approx (2p - 1)K$, i.e. λ is close to the lower bound, setting $\phi = 1$ is optimal. While, $\lambda \approx K[p + \sqrt{p(1-p)}]$, i.e. λ close to upper bound, is pointing toward the case when having only foreign currency debt by banks is optimal, given that the more nominal bonds there are in banks debtholding, the higher the inflationary-bias.

We should emphasize that the levels of λ (the marginal cost of taxation) are related to the levels of α as captured by the term $K = (1-\beta)\frac{A_H - (1+r^*)}{(1+r^*) - \alpha A_H}$ before. Since the higher α is, the higher K is, we see the point of what lies at the roots of the inflationary process. A greater efficiency (higher α) of the banking system enables banks to increase their leverage to expand investment in the economy's productive sector. Consequently, balance-sheet effects become stronger, and the adverse impact of higher inflation on investment increases in α, as captured by the term $\frac{(1+r^{*})}{(1+r^{*})-\alpha A_{H}}$ from (14). The higher α also enhances debt sustainability by increasing banks' ability to raise deposits to expand public bondholdings at $t = 0$ and, as a result, increasing banks' exposure to public debt. The intuition behind this result is that a higher level of financial institution development limits the inflationary-bias since the total costs of such a strategy for society may be high.

3.5. CONCLUSION

Our model explores the observed positive association between financial development, low inflation and domestic currency denominated debt. In our setting, the origins of the inflationary-bias lie either in the public debt composition (through the term ϕ), but also in the institutions themselves (through the term α). Indeed, inflation both reduces the ex-post real value of nominal debt and can additionally redistribute wealth between domestic agents (savers and bankers). In particular, lower-than-expected inflation may redistribute wealth in favour of bankers if they hold a share of domestic public debt denominated in domestic currency larger than average (and larger than the amount of domestic currency deposits of savers) in equilibrium. Hence, in our model, the government faces two inflation-related incentives. As in a traditional Barro-Gordon model, the government has an incentive to inflate the nominal debt away in order to reduce the burden of distortionary conventional taxation. In addition, the government has an incentive to set lower-than-expected inflation in high productivity states in order to redistribute wealth in favour of bankers (when they hold most of the nominal debt) and, thus, stimulate investment and growth. In this case, the costs of greater (on average) expected inflation are traded off with the gain from more investment in the high productive state. Otherwise stated, in the case of high productivity at $t = 1$, for any given level of domestic debt, the greater the share of nominal debt held by banks, the lower the incentive to inflate. The incentive of government to redistribute in favour of banks increases with financial development (through the term α), i.e. with the amount of resources intermediated by the banking sector. More specifically on this point, the more efficient banks are (the higher α is), the lower inflation is for any level of nominal domestic debt and for any distribution of domestic debt between bankers and savers. A higher level of financial development allows banks to increase their leverage, thereby attracting more deposits to expand investment in the economy's productive sector. Consequently, balance-sheet effects become stronger, and the adverse impact of higher inflation on investment increases in α, as captured by the term $\frac{1+r^*}{(1+r^*)-\alpha A_H}$ from (14). Higher α also enhances debt sustainability by increasing banks' ability to raise deposits to expand public bondholdings at $t=0$ and, as a result, increasing banks' exposure to public debt. The intuition behind this result is that a higher level of financial institution development limits the inflationary-bias since the total costs of such a strategy for society may be high.

On the other hand, the government's motivation to inflate is high in the low productive state. Indeed, inflation is independent of the distribution of debt between banks and savers. It only depends on the amount of total nominal debt in the low productive state. Inflation would be zero, $\pi=0$, if all the debt were denominated in foreign currency, while inflationary-bias increases by the amount of nominal debt.

We show that, in financially less-developed and under-productive economies, when redistribution effects are unimportant, the government finds it optimal to issue inflation-indexed debt (or foreign currency debt) to reduce the inflationary-bias. Conversely, in more efficient systems (which allow banks to be more leveraged and redistribution becomes an important source of financing productive investment), the government issues domestic debt and lowers inflation in states of nature when productivity is high in order to redistribute wealth in favor of banks, thereby enhancing investment and growth. Diverging from the conventional wisdom, our findings suggest that it is the development of the banking sectors that leads to lower inflation and not the other way around. Hence, the model can explain why financial development, i.e. an efficient banking sector, is instrumental to the creation of a domestic bond market and why such development is associated with lower equilibrium inflation.

APPENDICES

APPENDIX I. LIST OF COUNTRIES

Low-income countries: Burundi, Benin, Bangladesh, Central African Republic, Côte d'Ivoire, Eritrea, Ethiopia, Ghana, Guinea, Gambia, Guinea-Bissau, Haiti, Kenya, Kyrgyz Republic, Cambodia, Lao PDR, Liberia, Madagascar, Mali, Myanmar, Mozambique, Mauritania, Malawi, Niger, Nigeria, Nepal, Pakistan, Papua New Guinea, Rwanda, Senegal, Solomon Islands, Sierra Leone, Chad, Togo, Tajikistan, Uganda, Uzbekistan, Vietnam, Yemen, Rep., Congo, Dem. Rep., Zambia, Zimbabwe.

Middle-income countries: Albania, Argentina, Armenia, Azerbaijan, Bulgaria, Bosnia and Herzegovina, Belarus, Belize, Bolivia, Brazil, Bhutan, Botswana, Chile, China, Cameroon, Congo Rep., Colombia, Cape Verde, Costa Rica, Djibouti, Dominica, Dominican Republic, Algeria, Ecuador, Egypt Arab Rep., Fiji, Micronesia Fed. Sts., Gabon, Georgia, Grenada, Guatemala, Guyana, Honduras, Croatia, Indonesia, India, Iran Islamic Rep., Jamaica, Jordan, Kazakhstan, Kiribati, St. Kitts and Nevis, Lebanon, Libya, St. Lucia, Sri Lanka, Lesotho, Lithuania, Latvia, Morocco, Moldova, Maldives, Mexico, Marshall Islands, Macedonia FYR, Montenegro, Mongolia, Mauritius, Malaysia, Namibia, Nicaragua, Panama, Peru, Philippines, Palau, Poland, Paraguay, Romania, Russian Federation, Sudan, El Salvador, Serbia, Suriname, Swaziland, Seychelles, Syrian Arab Republic, Thailand, Turkmenistan, Timor-Leste, Tonga, Tunisia, Turkey, Ukraine, Uruguay, St. Vincent and the Grenadines, Venezuela RB., Vanuatu, West Bank and Gaza, Samoa, South Africa.

High-income countries: Australia, Austria, Belgium, Bahrain, Bahamas, Bermuda, Barbados, Brunei Darussalam, Canada, Switzerland, Channel Islands, Cyprus, Czech Republic, Germany, Denmark, Spain, Estonia, Finland, France, United Kingdom, Equatorial Guinea, Greece, Hong Kong China,

Hungary, Ireland, Iceland, Israel, Italy, Japan, Korea Rep., Kuwait, Luxembourg, Macao China, Malta, Netherlands, Norway, New Zealand, Oman, Puerto Rico, Portugal, Singapore, Slovak Republic, Slovenia, Sweden, Trinidad and Tobago, United States.

APPENDIX II. GROWTH REGRESSIONS

Table 1. FE results for Total debt/GDP, by subsamples

	Dependent variable: "Per capita GDP growth", FE								
	Middle-income	2. Middle-income	3.Middle-income	4.Low-income	5. Low-income	6.Low-income	7. High-income	8. High-income	9. High-income
L. Total debt/GDP	0.069***	0.062***	0.072***	0.050**	0.069***	0.069***	0.038	0.016	0.014
	(0.025)	(0.023)	(0.026)	(0.022)	(0.021)	(0.020)	(0.030)	(0.033)	(0.033)
[L. Total debt/GDP]^2	-0.018***	-0.016***	-0.019***	-0.011**	-0.018***	-0.018***	-0.001	0.022	0.022
	(0.007)	(0.006)	(0.007)	(0.005)	(0.005)	(0.005)	(0.018)	(0.022)	(0.022)
L. External debt/Total debt		-0.015			0.005			-0.035***	
		(0.018)			(0.043)			(0.014)	
L. Domestic debt/Total debt			-0.015			-0.021			0.025*
			(0.026)			(0.035)			(0.013)
Log Initial per capita GDP	-0.029	-0.039	-0.025	-0.061**	-0.098*	-0.092*	-0.029	-0.028	-0.029
	(0.023)	(0.028)	(0.027)	(0.027)	(0.054)	(0.052)	(0.020)	(0.023)	(0.024)
Population growth	-0.304	-0.284	-0.318	0.571	0.110	0.105	-0.365**	-0.321*	-0.356**
	(0.228)	(0.233)	(0.229)	(0.444)	(0.097)	(0.098)	(0.172)	(0.172)	(0.180)
Log Inflation	-0.005**	-0.005*	-0.005**	-0.014***	-0.012*	-0.012*	-0.006***	-0.007***	-0.007***
	(0.002)	(0.002)	(0.002)	(0.005)	(0.006)	(0.006)	(0.001)	(0.002)	(0.002)
L. LLY	-0.035	-0.032	-0.035	0.152***	0.117**	0.119**	-0.001	-0.002	-0.003
	(0.041)	(0.039)	(0.041)	(0.041)	(0.049)	(0.051)	(0.010)	(0.013)	(0.014)
L. MCAP	0.022***	0.022***	0.022***				0.010***	0.012**	0.011*
	(0.008)	(0.008)	(0.008)				(0.003)	(0.005)	(0.005)
L. Savings rate	0.014***	0.014***	0.013***	0.006	0.010	0.001	0.011***	0.011*	0.010*
	(0.005)	(0.005)	(0.005)	(0.005)	(0.005)	(0.005)	(0.004)	(0.005)	(0.054)
L. Trade openness	0.004	0.005	0.004	0.010	-0.004	-0.004	0.002**	0.018	0.002**
	(0.002)	(0.003)	(0.002)	(0.002)	(0.030)	(0.029)	(0.001)	(0.012)	(0.001)
L. Risk index (ICRG)	0.012***	0.012***	0.012***		0.012	0.011	0.013***	0.012**	0.012**
	(0.003)	(0.003)	(0.003)		(0.007)	(0.007)	(0.004)	(0.005)	(0.006)
Constant	0.105	0.187	0.075	0.286*	0.454	0.432	0.136	0.155	0.140
	(0.161)	(0.206)	(0.189)	(0.161)	(0.288)	(0.262)	(0.199)	(0.229)	(0.233)
Overall R^2	0.04	0.04	0.05	0.10	0.04	0.03	0.13	0.10	0.14
Within R^2	0.13	0.13	0.13	0.23	0.16	0.17	0.23	0.22	0.21
Between R^2	0.00	0.00	0.00	0.08	0.00	0.00	0.17	0.16	0.29
N	542	541	541	325	210	210	501	384	384

(*) Indicates marginal significance at the 10%-level, (**) at the 5%-level, (***) at the 1%-level. Robust standard errors are reported below the estimated parameters.

Table 2. GMM results for Total debt/GDP, by subsamples

Dependent variable: "PPP GDP growth", GMM (2-step)

	1. Middle-income	2. Middle-income	3. Middle-income	4. Middle-income	5. Low-income	6.Low-income	7.Low-income	8.High income
L. Total debt/GDP	0.482** (0.202)	0.410** (0.186)	0.511*** (0.197)	0.447*** (0.177)	0.176* (0.102)	0.071* (0.040)	0.157* (0.085)	0.010 (0.762)
[L. Total debt/GDP]^2	-0.282* (0.162)	-0.240* (0.153)	-0.304** (0.156)	-0.266*(0.153)	-0.129* (0.089)	-0.030 (0.061)	-0.099* (0.090)	-0.011 (0.083)
HD* [L. Total debt/GDP]	-0.195 (0.126)	-0.166 (0.123)	-0.211* (0.123)		-0.109 (0.078)	-0.010 (0.038)	-0.077 (0.068)	-0.067 (0.096)
HD*[L. Total debt/GDP]^2	0.206 (0.144)	0.176 (0.139)	0.225 (0.139)		0.110 (0.084)	0.011 (0.059)	0.077 (0.087)	0.067 (0.108)
MD*[L. Total debt/GDP]^2				0.004 (0.012)				
L. External debt/Total debt		-0.058** (0.030)				0.110 (0.069)		
L. Domestic debt/Total debt			0.033 (0.039)				-0.142* (0.077)	
Log Initial per capita GDP	-0.054 (0.075)	-0.121 (0.078)	-0.066 (0.096)	-0.075 (0.058)	-0.015***(0.005)	-0.031**(0.013)	-0.017***(0.003)	0.007 (0.041)
Population growth	0.016 (0.221)	-0.457 (0.602)	0.007 (0.276)	0.097 (0.325)	0.503 (0.604)	0.369 (0.415)	0.387 (0.609)	-0.258 (0.386)
Log Inflation	-0.010*** (0.002)	-0.010*** (0.003)	-0.010*** (0.002)	-0.010*** (0.003)	-0.006* (0.003)	-0.001 (0.006)	-0.002 (0.580)	-0.003 (0.002)
L. LLY	-0.016 (0.113)	0.011 (0.117)	-0.051 (0.121)	-0.157 (0.064)	0.082 (0.088)	0.432 (0.254)	0.427**(0.210)	-0.011 (0.016)
L. MCAP	0.049*** (0.019)	0.047** (0.022)	0.051** (0.021)	0.049*** (0.017)				-0.007 (0.006)
L. Savings rate	0.011 (0.006)	0.011 (0.006)	0.010 (0.007)	0.014** (0.007)	0.003 (0.008)	0.013 (0.009)	0.011 (0.006)	-0.001 (0.038)
L. Trade openness	0.011*** (0.004)	0.012*** (0.004)	0.012*** (0.004)	0.015*** (0.003)	0.003 (0.002)	-0.004 (0.002)	-0.004 (0.003)	0.014** (0.006)
L. Risk index (ICRG)	0.006 (0.009)	0.007 (0.009)	0.008 (0.010)	0.010 (0.008)		-0.011 (0.014)	-0.007 (0.011)	0.002 (0.004)
L. PPP GDP growth	-0.143 (0.119)	-0.156 (0.097)	-0.189 (0.120)	-0.263**(0.104)	0.178 (0.234)	0.411 (0.417)	0.389 (0.420)	0.348***(0.116)
L.R. effect of Total debt/GDP	0.422**(0.176)	0.354**(0.165)	0.429***(0.163)	0.354** (0.151)	0.214* (0.109)	0.122 (0.111)	0.258 (0.244)	0.001 (0.116)
L.R. effect of [Total debt/GDP]^2	-0.247*(0.140)	-0.208 (0.135)	-0.256**(0.129)	-0.211 (0.127)	-0.157 (0.096)	-0.051 (0.116)	-0.163 (0.207)	-0.017 (0.128)
L.R. effect of External/Total debt		-0.050* (0.026)						
L.R. effect of Domestic /Total debt			0.028 (0.032)					
L.R. effect of LLY	-0.014(0.098)	0.010 (0.102)	-0.042 (0.100)	-0.125 (0.047)	0.099 (0.116)	0.735 (0.769)	0.700 (0.643)	-0.016 (0.026)

Table 2. (Continued)

	1. Middle-income	2. Middle-income	3. Middle-income	4. Middle-income	5. Low-income	6.Low-income	7.Low-income	8.High income
L.R. effect of MCAP	0.042**(0.018)	0.041**(0.020)	0.043**(0.019)	0.039***(0.014)				-0.011 (0.010)
L.R. effect of Trade openness	0.010***(0.003)	0.010***(0.003)	0.010***(0.003)	0.012*** (0.002)	0.004 (0.003)	-0.006 (0.008)	-0.007 (0.009)	0.021* (0.011)
L.R. effect of Inflation	-0.010***(0.002)	- 0.010***(0.002)	- 0.010***(0.002)	-0.008***(0.002)	-0.007** (0.003)	-0.002 (0.009)	-0.004 (0.948)	-0.004 (0.003)
L.R. effect of Initial PPP GDP	-0.048(0.065)	-0.105 (0.067)	-0.056 (0.081)	-0.059 (0.046)	-0.018**(0.008)	-0.053 (0.048)	-0.029 (0.018)	0.001 (0.006)
L.R. effect of Risk index	0.005(0.008)	0.006 (0.008)	0.006 (0.008)	0.008 (0.006)		-0.018 (0.033)	-0.011 (0.023)	0.003 (0.007)
Total debt turning point	**0.854***(0.153)**	**0.853***(0.184)**	**0.840***(0.128)**	**0.839***(0.180)**	**0.679***(0.124)**	-	**0.792** (0.333)**	-
Arellano-Bond AR(2): Prob>z	0.636	0.815	0.564	0.304	0.858	0.574	0.574	0.774
Hansen test of over.restr.: Prob>chi2	0.998	0.915	0.896	0.921	1.000	1.000	1.000	1.000
N of observations	481	480	480	428	321	202	202	476

Notes: Specification choice: GMM

(i) GMM results obtained using STATA's xtabond2 command, (ii) t- statistics for GMM are heteroskedasticity-consistent, (iii) Arellano-bond AR(2) tests is for 2nd –order serial correlation in errors. 1st order serial correlation is expected; model identification requires absence of 2nd order correlation, (iv) GMM instrumentation: Financial development indicators are treated as endogenous, "law and order" is used as external instruments(iv-style instruments), (v) Instruments used for differenced equation: X_{t-2}, where X denotes endogenous variable, (vi)Windmeijer-corrected cluster-robust errors are reported along the estimated parameters.

(*) Indicates marginal significance at the 10%-level, (**) at the 5%-level, (***) at the 1%-level. Robust standard errors are reported along the estimated parameters

Table 3. GMM and FE results for External/Domestic debt shares, High- income sample

Dependent variable: "PPP GDP growth", GMM, 2-step

	1. GMM	2. FE	3. GMM	4. FE
L. External debt/GDP	0.047 (0.322)	0.136* (0.078)		
[L. External debt/GDP]^2	-0.105 (0.700)	-0.151 (0.120)		
L. Domestic debt/GDP			0.004 (0.046)	0.054 (0.036)
[L. Domestic debt/GDP]^2			-0.010 (0.043)	0.002 (0.030)
HFD* [L. Domestic debt/GDP]			-0.016 (0.022)	
L. External debt/Total debt	0.007 (0.022)	-0.067***(0.022)		
Log Initial per capita GDP	-0.002 (0.011)	-0.028 (0.021)	-0.003 (0.051)	-0.027 (0.024)
Population growth	-0.047 (0.633)	-0.293* (0.172)	-0.078 (0.389)	-0.328* (0.174)
Log Inflation	-0.003 (0.003)	-0.006** (0.002)	-0.003 (0.002)	-0.006***(0.002)
L. LLY	-0.011 (0.030)	-0.007 (0.017)	-0.008 (0.023)	-0.006 (0.014)
L. MCAP	-0.004 (0.007)	0.013***(0.005)	-0.004 (0.005)	0.011**(0.005)
L. Savings rate	0.029 (0.063)	0.090 (0.065)	0.001 (0.005)	0.009 (0.006)
L. Trade openness	0.010 (0.010)	0.012 (0.016)	0.013***(0.005)	0.022 (0.013)
L. Risk index (ICRG)	0.037 (0.080)	0.105** (0.052)	0.023 (0.055)	0.121** (0.057)
L.R. effect of External debt/GDP	0.065 (0.447)			
L.R. effect of [External debt/GDP]^2	-0.146 (0.972)			
L.R. effect of Domestic debt/GDP			0.006 (0.068)	
L.R. effect of External/Total debt	0.010 (0.031)			
L.R. effect of Domestic /Total debt				
L.R. effect of LLY	-0.015 (0.042)		-0.012 (0.035)	
L.R. effect of MCAP	-0.005 (0.011)		-0.006 (0.008)	
L.R. effect of Trade openness	0.015 (0.015)		0.020***(0.007)	
L.R. effect of Inflation	-0.004 (0.004)		-0.004 (0.003)	
L.R. effect of Initial PPP GDP	-0.003 (0.015)		-0.005 (0.076)	
External debt turning point	-		-	
Arellano-Bond AR(2): Prob>z	0.133		0.165	
Hansen test of over.restr.:Prob>chi2	1.000		1.000	
Overall R^2		0.11		0.14
Within R^2		0.21		0.21
N of observations	363	384	363	384

(*) Indicates marginal significance at the 10%-level, (**) at the 5%-level, (***) at the 1%-level. Robust standard errors are reported along the estimated parameters

Table 4. GMM and FE results for External/Domestic debt shares, Middle-income sample

Dependent variable: "PPP GDP growth", GMM (2-step)

	1. GMM	2. FE	3. GMM	4. FE	5. GMM	6. FE	7. GMM	8. FE
L. External debt/GDP	0.312** (0.143)	0.139*** (0.046)	0.243* (0.141)	0.104*** (0.038)				
[L. External debt/GDP]^2	-0.216* (0.117)	-0.100** (0.050)	-0.166 (0.121)	-0.077* (0.042)				
HD* [L. External debt/GDP]	-0.172* (0.092)	-0.057 (0.058)	-0.142 (0.103)	-0.047 (0.0549				
HD*[L. External debt/GDP]^2	0.175 (0.105)	0.074 (0.053)	0.142 (0.112)	0.061 (0.047)				
L. Domestic debt/GDP					0.365** (0.173)	0.026 (0.075)	0.269 (0.190)	-0.004 (0.066)
[L. Domestic debt/GDP]^2					-0.338 (0.208)	0.015 (0.086)	-0.245 (0.223)	0.044 (0.078)
HFD* [L. Domestic debt/GDP]					-0.303 (0.187)	-0.038 (0.052)	-0.288 (0.199)	-0.042 (0.053)
HFD*[L. Domestic debt/GDP]^2					0.682 (0.440)	0.109 (0.106)	0.634 (0.459)	0.103 (0.108)
L. External debt/Total debt	-0.133*** (0.045)	-0.043** (0.021)					-0.056***(0.023)	-0.020 (0.015)
L. Domestic debt/Total debt			0.089* (0.049)	0.004 (0.024)				
Log Initial per capita GDP	-0.157* (0.085)	-0.037 (0.028)	-0.127 (0.084)	-0.025 (0.029)	-0.167*** (0.061)	-0.049**(0.022)	-0.233***(0.081)	-0.059**(0.026)
Population growth	-0.092 (0.781)	-0.284 (0.239)	0.398 (0.842)	-0.379 (0.231)	-0.091 (0.522)	-0.357 (0.233)	0.094 (0.272)	-0.343 (0.233)
Log Inflation	-0.010*** (0.003)	-0.005** (0.002)	-0.010*** (0.002)	-0.005** (0.002)	-0.009*** (0.003)	-0.004 (0.002)	-0.010***(0.003)	-0.004 (0.002)
L. LLY	0.065 (0.126)	-0.031 (0.039)	-0.008 (0.141)	-0.031 (0.042)	0.124 (0.139)	-0.020 (0.046)	0.174 (0.163)	-0.017 (0.045)
L. MCAP	0.058** (0.026)	0.021***(0.008)	0.071*** (0.026)	0.021*** (0.008)	0.052*** (0.020)	0.019***(0.007)	0.064** (0.029)	0.020***(0.006)
L. Savings rate	0.013** (0.006)	0.014*** (0.005)	0.008 (0.006)	0.014*** (0.005)	0.013** (0.006)	0.012***(0.004)	0.013 (0.008)	0.014***(0.004)
L. Trade openness	0.011*** (0.004)	0.005 (0.003)	0.012*** (0.004)	0.004 (0.002)	0.010** (0.004)	0.005 (0.003)	0.011***(0.004)	0.005*(0.003)
L. Risk index (ICRG)	0.002 (0.010)	0.013*** (0.003)	0.003 (0.009)	0.011*** (0.004)	0.005 (0.082)	0.010***(0.003)	-0.010 (0.094)	0.010***(0.003)
LR. effect of External debt/GDP	0.284**(0.138)		0.221 (0.130)					
LR. effect of [External debt/GDP]^2	-0.196*(0.111)		-0.150 (0.111)					
LR. effect of Domestic debt/GDP					0.340**(0.154)		0.251 (0.163)	
LR. effect of External/Total debt	-0.121***(0.042)						-0.052*** (0.021)	
LR. effect of Domestic /Total debt			0.081*(0.045)					
LR. effect of LLY	0.059 (0.116)		-0.007 (0.128)		0.116 (0.135)		0.162 (0.165)	
LR. effect of MCAP	0.053**(0.026)		0.064***(0.025)		0.049**(0.020)		0.060* (0.033)	
LR. effect of Trade openness	0.010***(0.003)		0.011***(0.004)		0.010***(0.003)		0.011***(0.003)	
LR. effect of Inflation	-0.010**(0.003)		-0.010***(0.002)		-0.010***(0.003)		-0.010**(0.003)	
LR. effect of Initial PPP GDP	-0.143*(0.076)		-0.115 (0.076)		-0.156***(0.061)		-0.217**(0.093)	
External debt turning point	0.725***(0.147)		0.734***(0.184)		-		-	
Arellano-Bond AR(2): Prob>z	0.742		0.640		0.678		0.732	
Hansen test of over.restr.:Prob>chi2	0.998		0.926		0.999		0.920	
Overall R^2		0.04		0.05		0.04		0.04
Within R^2		0.14		0.11		0.11		0.12
N of observations	480	541	480	541	482	543	480	541

(*) Indicates marginal significance at the 10%-level, (**) at the 5%-level, (***) at the 1%-level. Robust standard errors are reported along the estimated parameters.

Table 5. GMM and FE results for External/Domestic debt shares, Low-income sample

Dependent variable: "PPP GDP growth", GMM (2-step), FE

	1. GMM	2. FE	3. GMM	4. FE	5. GMM	6. FE	7. GMM	8. FE
L. External debt/GDP	0.552* (0.307)	0.074** (0.036)	0.522** (0.226)	0.071** (0.034)	0.105** (0.050)	0.073**(0.034)		
[L. External debt/GDP]^2	-0.451* (0.292)	-0.024**(0.011)	-0.431* (0.217)	-0.023** (0.011	-0.885* (0.448)	-0.024** (0.011)		
HD* [L. External debt/GDP]	-0.382 (0.262)		-0.368* (0.194)		-0.759* (0.381)			
HD*[L. External debt/GDP]^2	0.401 (0.284)		0.385* (0.210)		0.809* (0.421)			
L. Domestic debt/GDP					-0.037 (0.056)	0.031 (0.0.053)	0.005 (0.018)	0.027* (0.014)
[L. Domestic debt/GDP]^2					-0.011 (0.074)	-0.041 (0.060)		
HFD* [L. Domestic debt/GDP]							-0.196***(0.060)	-0.088***(0.030)
HFD*[L. Domestic debt/GDP]^2								
L. External debt/Total debt	0.030 (0.086)	-0.016 (0.036)						
L. Domestic debt/Total debt			-0.102 (0.072)	-0.004 (0.027)				
Log Initial per capita GDP	-0.037***(0.013)	-0.090* (0.046)	-0.030***(0.010)	-0.087* (0.046)	-0.048***(0.016)	-0.093* (0.048)	-0.010* (0.005)	-0.109***(0.033)
Population growth	0.145 (0.095)	0.105 (0.093)	0.122* (0.066)	0.097 (0.093)	0.166 (0.107)	0.104 (0.090)	0.035 (0.055)	0.104 (0.094)
Log Inflation	-0.003 (0.005)	-0.012 (0.007)	-0.002 (0.004)	-0.011 (0.007)	-0.006 (0.003)	-0.012 (0.007)	-0.007* (0.004)	-0.009 (0.006)
L. LLY	0.262 (0.279)	0.124** (0.052)	0.324 (0.212)	0.128** (0.054)	0.138 (0.110)	0.123** (0.054)	0.280*** (0.103)	0.188***(0.069)
L. Savings rate	0.005 (0.006)	-0.003 (0.005)	0.008 (0.005)	-0.002 (0.005)	0.007 (0.005)	-0.001 (0.006)	0.002 (0.040)	-0.003 (0.006)
L. Trade openness	-0.002 (0.027)	-0.001 (0.027)	-0.010 (0.025)	0.001 (0.027)	0.010 (0.029)	0.001 (0.027)	-0.005** (0.001)	-0.001 (0.033)
L. Risk index (ICRG)	-0.027 (0.131)	0.011 (0.007)	-0.003 (0.010)	0.011 (0.007)	-0.005 (0.070)	0.011 (0.007)	0.007 (0.004)	0.013* (0.007)
LR. effect of External debt/GDP	0.537*(0.286)		0.509** (0.238)		0.906* (0.458)			
LR. effect of [External debt/GDP]^2	-0.439* (0.265)		-0.421* (0.220)		-0.764* (0.409)			
LR. HFD* [L. Domestic debt/GDP]							-0.175***(0.036)	
LR. effect of External/Total debt								
LR. effect of Domestic /Total debt								
LR. effect of LLY	0.255 (0.306)		0.316 (0.207)		0.119***(0.030)		0.249*** (0.076)	
LR. effect of Trade openness	-0.002 (0.027)		-0.010 (0.002)		0.007 (0.024)		-0.004***(0.001)	
LR. effect of Inflation	-0.003 (0.004)		-0.001 (0.004)		-0.005* (0.002)		-0.007**(0.002)	
LR. effect of Initial PPP GDP	-0.036** (0.017)		-0.029** (0.012)		-0.042*** (0.015)		-0.008 (0.005)	
LR. effect of Risk index	-0.026 (0.130)		-0.003 (0.009)		-0.005 (0.005)		0.007 (0.004)	
External debt turning point	0.611*** (0.060)		0.605*** (0.050)		0.592*** (0.024)			
Arellano-Bond AR(2): Prob>z	0.901		0.925		0.887		0.547	
Hansen test of over.restr.:Prob>chi2	1.000		1.000		1.000		1.000	
Overall R^2		0.03		0.03		0.03		
Within R^2		0.16		0.16		0.16		
Between R^2		0.00		0.00		0.00		
N of observations	202	210	202	210	202	210	203	211

(*) Indicates marginal significance at the 10%-level, (**) at the 5%-level, (***) at the 1%-level. Robust standard errors are reported along the estimated parameters.

APPENDIX III. FIXED EFFECT RESULTS

Table 1. Fixed effect results using information on LLY and MCAP to measure financial development

	Dependent variable: "Domestic-to-Total debt", FE, Medium income sample								
	1	2	3	4	5	6	7	8	9
Inflation	-0.106	-0.056	-0.040	-0.019	-0.027	-0.012	0.006	-0.021	0.008
	(0.019)***	(0.026)**	(0.031)	(0.031)	(0.032)	(0.035)	(0.051)	(0.036)	(0.067)
LLY		0.358	0.407	0.452	0.442	0.373	0.379	0.497	0.333
		(0.115)***	(0.178)**	(0.154)***	(0.157)***	(0.130)***	(0.144)**	(0.164)***	(0.155)**
MCAP			0.076	0.077	0.082	0.065	0.097	0.069	0.092
			(0.023)***	(0.028)***	(0.027)***	(0.031)**	(0.050)*	(0.023)***	(0.050)*
Total debt/GDP	0.080	0.028	0.017	-0.017	-0.011	-0.093	-0.051	0.037	0.016
	(0.323)	(0.029)	(0.029)	(0.024)	(0.024)	(0.233)	(0.593)	(0.037)	(0.074)
Law and Order				-0.051	-0.048	-0.036	-0.019		
				(0.018)***	(0.018)***	(0.015)**	(0.015)		
Savings rate					0.029	0.033	0.057		0.055
					(0.019)	(0.019)*	(0.026)**		(0.028)*
Trade openness						0.011	0.002		0.005
						(0.011)	(0.008)		(0.009)
Government Stability						0.081	0.049		
						(0.054)	(0.042)		
Quality of Bureaucracy						-0.014	-0.025		
						(0.032)	(0.026)		
Exchange rate volatility							-0.021		-0.013
							(0.027)		(0.025)
Risk index (ICRG)								0.031	0.016
								(0.017)*	(0.017)
Constant	0.360	0.181	0.202	0.369	0.302	0.160	0.161	-0.077	-0.045
	(0.018)***	(0.058)***	(0.085)**	(0.079)***	(0.092)***	(0.105)	(0.112)	(0.143)	(0.186)
N	873	798	531	479	478	468	228	479	228
Overall R^2	0.001	0.08	0.18	0.20	0.22	0.13	0.40	0.15	0.35

(*) Indicates marginal significance at the 10%-level, (**) at the 5%-level, (***) at the 1%-level. Robust standard errors are reported below the estimated parameters.

Table 2. Fixed effect results using information on LLY and MCAP to measure financial development (by subsamples)

Dependent variable: "Domestic-to-Total debt", FE

	"High income" group 1	"Middle income" group 2	"Low income" group 3	"High income" group 4	"Middle income" Group 5	"Low income" group 6	"High income" group 7	"Middle income" Group 8	"Low income" group 9	"High income" group 10	"Middle income" Group 11
Inflation	-0.015	-0.012	0.016	-0.012	0.006	-0.003	-0.014	-0.021	-0.404	-0.012	0.008
	(0.005)***	(0.035)	(0.017)	(0.003)***	(0.051)	(0.011)	(0.003)***	(0.036)	(0.945)	(0.003)***	(0.067)
LLY	0.058	0.373	0.628	-0.069	0.379	0.003	0.039	0.497	0.053	-0.046	0.333
	(0.114)	(0.130)***	(0.307)*	(0.129)	(0.144)**	(0.199)	(0.088)	(0.164)***	(0.231)	(0.124)	(0.155)**
MCAP	0.011	0.065	0.547	-0.022	0.097		-0.029	0.069		-0.043	0.092
	(0.352)	(0.031)**	(0.134)***	(0.028)	(0.050)*		(0.026)	(0.023)***		(0.032)	(0.050)*
Total debt/ GDP	0.040	-0.093	0.064	0.027	-0.051	0.045	0.038	0.037	0.039	0.033	0.016
	(0.173)	(0.233)	(0.137)	(0.159)	(0.593)	(0.016)	(0.125)	(0.037)	(0.016)**	(0.154)	(0.074)
Law and Order	0.010	-0.036	-0.048	-0.008	-0.019	-0.015					
	(0.025)	(0.015)**	(0.023)*	(0.026)	(0.015)	(0.035)					
Savings rate	0.072	0.033	-0.024	-0.033	0.057	0.029			0.025	-0.045	0.055
	(0.055)	(0.019)*	(0.041)	(0.040)	(0.026)**	(0.016)*			(0.017)	(0.039)	(0.028)*
Trade openness	-0.077	0.011	0.006	0.060	0.002	0.069			0.083	0.007	0.005
	(0.920)	(0.011)	(0.015)	(0.070)	(0.008)	(0.072)			(0.077)	(0.007)	(0.009)
Government Stability	-0.012	0.081	0.012	-0.090	0.049	0.074					
	(0.006)*	(0.054)	(0.009)	(0.049)*	(0.042)	(0.073)					
Quality of Bureaucracy	-0.040	-0.014	-0.005	0.064	-0.025	-0.009					
	(0.606)	(0.032)	(0.024)	(0.060)	(0.026)	(0.021)					
Exchange rate volatility				-0.007	-0.021					0.017	-0.013
				(0.042)	(0.027)					(0.040)	(0.025)
Risk index							0.098	0.031	0.007	0.068	0.016
							(0.035)***	(0.017)*	(0.025)	(0.030)**	(0.017)
Constant	0.696	0.160	-0.034	0.708	0.161	0.109	-0.083	-0.077	0.058	0.265	-0.045
	(0.330)***	(0.105)	(0.271)	(0.352)**	(0.112)	(0.069)	(0.310)	(0.143)	(0.129)	(0.357)	(0.186)
N	311	468	84	274	228	186	326	479	186	274	228
Overall R^2	0.08	0.13	0.37	0.02	0.40	0.02	0.15	0.15	0.05	0.07	0.35

(*) Indicates marginal significance at the 10%-level, (**) at the 5%-level, (***) at the 1%-level. Robust standard errors are reported below the estimated parameters.

Table 3. Fixed effect results using information on PRIVO, BTOT and MCAP to measure financial development (by subsamples)

Dependent variable: "Domestic-to-Total debt", FE

	"High income" group 1	"Middle income" Group 2	"Low income" group 3	"High income" group 4	"Middle income" Group 5	"Low income" group 6	"High income" group 7	"Middle income" Group 8	"Low income" group 9	"High income" group 10	"Middle income" group 11	"Low income" group 12	"Middle income" group 13	"Middle income" Group 14
Inflation	-0.011	-0.034	-0.011	-0.011	-0.045	-0.424	-0.007	-0.016	-0.011	-0.080	0.018	-0.051	-0.033	-0.020
	(0.003)***	(0.031)	(0.007)	(0.003)***	(0.700)	(0.916)	(0.004)*	(0.054)	(0.010)	(0.038)**	(0.052)	(0.104)	(0.028)	(0.060)
PRIVO	-0.001	-0.148	0.737	0.029	0.175	0.218								
	(0.044)	(0.092)	(0.359)*	(0.428)	(0.102)	(0.403)								
BTOT							0.378	0.170	0.160	0.263	0.235	0.088	0.146	
							(0.219)*	(0.112)	(0.055)***	(0.216)	(0.123)*	(0.083)	(0.082)*	
MCAP	-0.031	0.098		-0.049			-0.014	0.114		-0.033				0.120
	(0.028)	(0.026)***		(0.030)			(0.028)	(0.064)*		(0.031)				(0.065)*
Total debt/GDP	0.044	-0.197	0.031	0.048	0.065	0.061	0.099	0.427	0.032	0.071	0.070	0.054	0.086	-0.095
	(0.170)	(0.223)	(0.050)	(0.166)	(0.062)	(0.058)	(0.164)	(0.614)	(0.048)	(0.161)	(0.057)	(0.050)	(0.354)	(0.447)
Law and Order	-0.008	-0.030	0.088				-0.001	-0.018	0.069				-0.017	-0.025
	(0.027)	(0.014)**	(0.019)***				(0.026)	(0.017)	(0.024)**				(0.014)	(0.016)
Savings rate	-0.029	0.039	0.024	-0.043	-0.012	0.014	-0.026	0.041	0.016	-0.039	-0.019	0.011	-0.054	0.049
	(0.037)	(0.025)**	(0.023)	(0.036)	(0.027)	(0.020)	(0.037)	(0.021)*	(0.021)	(0.036)	(0.024)	(0.018)	(0.156)	(0.023)**
Trade openness	0.006	0.021	0.041	0.077	0.012	-0.039	0.014	0.011	-0.019	0.026	0.014	-0.066	0.019	0.012
	(0.007)	(0.012)*	(0.057)	(0.071)	(0.009)	(0.068)	(0.071)	(0.007)	(0.072)	(0.068)	(0.009)	(0.067)	(0.008)**	(0.008)
Government Stability	-0.083	0.013	-0.061				-0.097	0.009	-0.061				0.048	0.091
	(0.046)*	(0.005)**	(0.047)				(0.047)**	(0.004)*	(0.051)				(0.040)	(0.045)**
Quality of Bureaucracy	0.064	-0.026	-0.007				0.078	-0.004	-0.006				-0.035	-0.038
	(0.061)	(0.032)	(0.017)				(0.056)	(0.028)	(0.017)				(0.023)	(0.280)
Exchange rate volatility	-0.076		-0.055	0.015	-0.015	-0.061	-0.047	-0.021	-0.037	0.018	-0.013	-0.052		-0.033
	(0.424)		(0.019)**	(0.041)	(0.019)	(0.026)**	(0.430)	(0.024)	(0.017)*	(0.041)	(0.022)	(0.024)*		(0.026)
Risk index				0.069	0.036	0.037				0.059	0.029	0.031		
				(0.029)**	(0.015)**	(0.015)**				(0.028)**	(0.014)**	(0.019)		
Constant	0.636	0.186	-0.128	0.202	-0.066	-0.023	0.177	0.042	-0.032	0.046	-0.133	0.012	0.201	0.218
	(0.323)**	(0.110)*	(0.105)	(0.316)	(0.163)	(0.081)	(0.396)	(0.147)	(0.103)	(0.383)	(0.160)	(0.09)	(0.107)*	(0.088**
N	278	468	104	278	302	104	274	251	104	274	327	104	643	251
Overall R^2	0.11	0.02	0.19	0.13	0.16	0.30	0.08	0.42	0.12	0.13	0.06	0.29	0.01	0.36

(*) Indicates marginal significance at the 10%-level, (**) at the 5%-level, (***) at the 1%-level. Corrected standard errors are reported below the estimated parameters.

Table 4. Fixed effect results using information on constructed indicators to measure financial development (by subsamples)

Dependent variable: "Domestic-to-Total debt", FE

	"High income" group	"Middle income" group	"High income" group	"Middle income" group	"High income" group	"Middle income" group	"Low income" group	"High income" group	"Middle income" group	"High income" group	"Middle income" group
	1	2	3	4	5	6	7	8	9	10	11
Inflation	-0.015	-0.467	-0.015	-0.626	-0.014	-0.050	-0.041	-0.014	-0.012	-0.015	-0.044
	(0.004)***	(0.774)	(0.003)***	(0.859)	(0.004)***	(0.048)	(0.094)	(0.003)***	(0.058)	(0.003)***	(0.032)
FD	0.014	0.060	-0.020	0.059							
	(0.023)	(0.012)***	(0.018)	(0.013)***							
FDEPTH					0.057	0.072	0.035	0.009	0.070		
					(0.036)	(0.026)***	(0.143)	(0.025)	(0.025)***		
FDEFF										-0.021	0.017
										(0.022)	(0.013)
Total debt/GDP	0.097	0.904	0.023	0.099	0.245	0.947	0.062	0.172	0.111	0.075	-0.123
	(0.208)	(0.678)	(0.198)	(0.069)	(0.207)	(0.575)	(0.067)	(0.187)	(0.064)*	(0.175)	(0.396)
Law and Order	0.011	-0.007			0.060	-0.006					-0.034
	(0.026)	(0.014)			(0.301)	(0.014)					(0.016)**
Savings rate	0.076	0.045	-0.042	0.044	0.084	-0.003	0.014	-0.030	-0.007	-0.054	0.031
	(0.055)	(0.025)*	(0.036)	(0.026)	(0.055)	(0.228)	(0.020)	(0.038)	(0.025)	(0.038)	(0.020)
Trade openness	-0.026	-0.007	0.035	-0.084	-0.015	0.069	-0.038	0.048	0.062	0.054	0.019
	(0.086)	(0.061)	(0.065)	(0.609)	(0.088)	(0.081)	(0.066)	(0.080)	(0.089)	(0.078)	(0.011)
Government Stability	-0.135	0.021			-0.105	0.024					0.124
	(0.080)	(0.046)			(0.059)*	(0.049)					(0.057)**
Quality of Bureaucracy	-0.035	-0.018			0.011	-0.031					-0.098
	(0.073)	(0.023)			(0.633)	(0.022)					(0.321)
Exchange rate volatility		0.095	0.052	0.014		-0.007	-0.058	0.024	-0.008	0.035	
		(0.220)	(0.428)	(0.021)		(0.018)	(0.026)**	(0.043)	(0.018)	(0.490)	
Risk index (ICRG)			0.053	0.058			0.036	0.060	0.031	0.067	
			(0.029)*	(0.186)			(0.020)	(0.033)*	(0.012)**	(0.034)*	
Constant	0.719	0.331	0.374	0.241	0.491	0.305	0.001	0.194	0.038	0.247	0.257
	(0.318)**	(0.113)***	(0.319)	(0.175)	(0.269)*	(0.104)***	(0.162)	(0.362)	(0.132)	(0.367)	(0.107)**
N	297	215	262	215	323	302	104	288	302	287	486
Overall R^2	0.10	0.49	0.11	0.48	0.16	0.16	0.22	0.17	0.20	0.20	0.18

(*) Indicates marginal significance at the 10%-level, (**) at the 5%-level, (***) at the 1%-level. Corrected standard errors are reported below the estimated parameters.

Table 5. Fixed effect results using information on constructed indicators to measure financial development (by subsamples)

Dependent variable: "Domestic-to-Total debt", FE

	"High income" group 1	"Middle income" group 2	"Low income" group 3	"High income" group 4	"Middle income" group 5	"Low income" group 6	"High income" group 7	"Middle income" Group 8	"Low income" group 9	"High income" group 10	"Middle income" Group 11
Inflation	-0.014	0.084	-0.024	-0.012	-0.104	0.026	-0.013	0.167	0.020	-0.013	-0.094
	(0.003)***	(0.052)	(0.075)	(0.004)***	(0.091)	(0.045)	(0.003)***	(0.095)*	(0.141)	(0.003)***	(0.612)
FDBANK	-0.001	0.067	0.003								
	(0.181)	(0.022)***	(0.026)								
FDSTOCK				-0.023	0.001	0.038				-0.023	
				(0.012)*	(0.152)	(0.015)**				(0.015)	
FDSIZE							-0.034	0.071	0.127		0.054
							(0.030)	(0.024)***	(0.057)**		(0.029)*
Total debt/GDP	0.145	0.055	0.055	-0.008	-0.046	0.058	0.019	0.026	0.055	-0.007	0.037
	(0.188)	(0.051)	(0.043)	(0.163)	(0.763)	(0.095)	(0.168)	(0.074)	(0.054)	(0.164)	(0.043)
Law and Order				-0.010	-0.059	-0.063					
				(0.024)	(0.150)	(0.037)					
Savings rate	-0.035	-0.028		-0.040	0.052		-0.048	0.058		-0.053	
	(0.037)	(0.250)		(0.037)	(0.023)**		(0.038)	(0.028)**		(0.036)	
Trade openness	0.051	0.039		0.005	0.015		0.067	0.005		0.005	
	(0.084)	(0.099)		(0.006)	(0.007)**		(0.071)	(0.006)		(0.006)	
Government Stability				-0.075	0.063						
				(0.037)**	(0.047)						
Quality of Bureaucracy				0.065	-0.023						
				(0.057)	(0.026)						
Exchange rate volatility	0.025	0.019		-0.023	-0.043		0.012	-0.011		-0.002	
	(0.044)	(0.025)		(0.039)	(0.026)		(0.039)	(0.026)		(0.040)	
Risk index (ICRG)	0.059	0.018	0.015				0.066	0.019	-0.046	0.057	0.029
	(0.033)*	(0.015)	(0.022)				(0.029)**	(0.016)	(0.039)	(0.025)**	(0.016)*
Constant	0.230	0.166	0.098	0.684	0.240	0.415	0.238	0.105	0.506	0.365	0.188
	(0.351)	(0.149)	(0.161)	(0.290)**	(0.100)**	(0.124)***	(0.297)	(0.149)	(0.233)	(0.278)	(0.123)
N	283	279	171	287	243	101	274	228	96	287	479
Overall R^2	0.17	0.25	0.13	0.13	0.19	0.39	0.10	0.36	0.27	0.17	0.21

(*) Indicates marginal significance at the 10%-level, (**) at the 5%-level, (***) at the 1%-level. Corrected standard errors are reported below the estimated parameters.

APPENDIX IV. SIMULTANEOUS EQUATIONS MODEL

Table 1. SEM results using information on LLY and MCAP to measure financial development (by subsamples)

Dependent variable: Domestic-to-Total debt and LLY, Simultaneous equations model

	"High income"		"Medium income"		"Low income"		"Medium income"		"Medium income"		"Low income"	
	1st eq.	2nd eq,	1st eq.	2nd eq.	1st eq.	2nd eq.	1st eq.	2nd eq.	1st eq.	2nd eq.	1st eq.	2nd eq.
Domestic-to-Total debt		0.201 (0.043)*** (4.61)		0.859 (0.103)*** (8.34)		0.163 (0.140) (1.16)		0.641 (0.084)*** (7.62)		0.859 (0.103)*** (8.34)		0.333 (0.139)*** (2.39)
LLY	0.163 (0.086)* (1.90)		0.667 (0.228)*** (2.92)		0.960 (0.549)* (1.75)		0.023 (0.140) (0.16)		0.658 (0.225)*** (2.92)		0.119 (0.038)*** (3.09)	
Inflation	-0.013 (0.003)*** (-3.98)	0.088 (0.090) (0.97)	0.028 (0.092) (0.31)	-0.066 (0.097) (-0.68)	0.134 (0.144) (0.92)	-0.186 (0.103)* (-1.79)	-0.271 (0.186) (-1.46))	-0.029 (0.169) (-0.17)		-0.066 (0.097) (-0.68)	0.222 (0.148) (1.49)	-0.132 (0.107) (-1.23)
MCAP	0.012 (0.035) (0.34)		0.101 (0.056)* (1.79)				0.258 (0.034)*** (7.39)		0.103 (0.055)* (1.85)			
Total debt/GDP	0.042 (0.038) (1.09)		-0.625 (0.593) (-1.05)		-0.721 (0.399)* (-1.81)		1.928 (0.854)** (2.26)		-0.603 (0.587) (-1.03)		-0.105 (0.042)*** (-2.51)	
Law and Order	0.002 (0.016) (0.11)			0.045 (0.011)*** (3.95)	-0.035 (0.023) (-1.51)			0.033 (0.011)*** (2.97)		0.045 (0.011)*** (3.95)		0.033 (0.014) (2.32)**
Savings rate	0.011 (0.015) (0.74)		0.041 (0.010)*** (4.00)		0.019 (0.032) (0.58)		0.029 0.021 (1.38)		0.041 (0.010)*** (4.03)		0.028 (0.017) (1.58)	
Trade openness		0.017 (0.003)*** (4.54)	-0.027 (0.005)*** (-4.57)	0.033 (0.002)*** (12.42)		0.029 (0.421) (0.07)		0.025 (0.003)*** (7.99)	-0.027 (0.005)*** (-4.59)	0.033 (0.002)*** (12.42)		0.052 (0.037) (1.38)
Government Stability	-0.022 (0.006)*** (-3.43)			0.072 (0.069) (1.03)	-0.026 (0.114) (-0.23)			0.015 (0.007)** (1.91)		0.007 (0.006) (1.03)		0.011 (0.005)* (1.79)
Quality of Bureaucracy	0.037 (0.023) (1.59)			-0.018 (0.023) (-0.75)				0.041 (0.022)* (1.83)		-0.018 (0.023) (-0.75)		0.021 (0.017) (1.24)
Exchange rate volatility					-0.056 (0.022)*** (-2.52)		-0.059 (0.037) (-1.57)				-0.037 (0.026) (-1.37)	
Risk index (ICRG)		0.015 (0.055) (0.28)	-0.043 (0.023)* (-1.83)			0.051 (0.018)*** (2.72)	0.019 (0.026) (0.75)		-0.043 (0.023)* (-1.83)		-0.037 (0.029) (-1.23)	
N	311	311	468	468	104	104	228	228	468	468	104	104
R^2	0.25	0.12	0.22	0.28	0.48	0.31	0.47	0.51	0.23	0.28	0.31	0.41
F–Stat	8.56	20.78	24.09	50.27	12.17	7.27	28.02	53.38	28.32	50.27	11.78	7.31
F-Stat. of joint null	3.28	6.91	11.05	6.93			12.58	28.90	11.23	5.42	7.96	3.76

(*) Indicates marginal significance at the 10%-level, (**) at the 5%-level, (***) at the 1%-level. Standard errors and t-statistics are reported below the estimated parameters.

Table 2. SEM results using information on BTOT and MCAP to measure financial development (by subsamples)

Dependent variable: Domestic-to-Total debt and BTOT, Simultaneous equations model

	"High income" group		"Medium income"		"Low income"		"Medium income"		"Medium income"		"Low income"	
	1st eq.	2nd eq,	1st eq.	2nd eq.	1st eq.	2nd eq.	1st eq.	2nd eq.	1st eq.	2nd eq.	1st eq.	2nd eq.
Domestic-to-Total debt		-0.029 (0.064) (-0.45)		0.255 (0.044)*** (5.71)		0.122 (0.253)*** (4.82)		0.278 (0.049)*** (5.66)		0.158 (0.037)*** (4.27)		0.182 (0.030)*** (6.08)
BTOT	0.091 (0.117) (0.78)		1.657 (0.788)** (2.10)		0.068 (0.148) (0.46)		1.555 (0.352)*** (4.41)		-0.100 (0.480) (-0.21)		0.474 (0.187)*** (2.52)	
Inflation	0.007 (0.212) (0.03)	-0.182 (0.016)*** (-10.78)	0.003 (0.237) (0.01)	-0.119 (0.103) (-1.15)	0.799 (0.385)** (2.07)	-0.356 (0.695) (-0.51)	-0.029 (0.203 (-0.14)	-0.186 (0.104)* (-1.79)	-0.035 (0.093) (-0.37)	-0.051 (0.045) (-1.12)	0.719 (0.437) (1.64)	-0.176 (0.075)** (-2.33)
MCAP	0.065 (0.025)*** (2.54)		0.166 (0.032)*** (5.18)				0.168 (0.029)*** (5.68)		0.205 (0.029)*** (6.90)			
Total debt/GDP	0.111 (0.611) (0.18)		0.333 (0.112)*** (2.96)		0.012 (0.184) (0.07)		3.039 (0.666)*** (4.56)		0.893 (0.477)* (1.87)		0.294 (0.194) (1.51)	
Law and Order		-0.065 (0.054) (-1.19)	-0.038 (0.216) (-0.18)		-0.019 (0.011) (-1.57)			0.093 (0.655) (0.14)	-0.020 (0.009)** (-2.21)			0.065 (0.219) (0.30)
Savings rate	-0.066 (0.019)*** (-3.38)		0.036 (0.024) (1.45)		0.048 (0.019)*** (2.46)		0.038 (0.016)*** (2.37)		0.056 (0.009)*** (5.71)		0.034 (0.019)* (1.73)	
Trade openness	0.079 (0.025)*** (3.15)	0.095 (0.073) (1.30)		-0.039 (0.017)** (-2.31)		0.025 (0.065) (0.38)		-0.411 (0.176)** (-2.32)	-0.012 (0.002)*** (-5.03)	0.014 (0.124) (0.11)	-0.075 (0.047) (-1.59)	0.012 (0.007) (1.57)
Government Stability		-0.018 (0.023) (-0.79)	-0.033 (0.010) (-0.30)		0.075 (0.065) (1.16)			0.044 (0.045) (0.96)	0.018 (0.006)*** (3.00)			0.058 (0.112) (0.52)
Quality of Bureaucracy		-0.052 (0.085) (-0.60)	-0.018 (0.041) (0.42)		0.026 (0.015)* (1.71)			0.026 (0.012)** (2.07)	0.083 (0.022)*** (3.67)			
Exchange rate volatility	-0.013 (0.332) (-0.04)		0.030 (0.070) (0.43)				0.024 (0.039) (0.62)					
Risk index (ICRG)	0.045 (0.021)** (2.11)			0.045 (0.012)*** (3.64)		0.010 (0.002)*** (3.69)	-0.015 (0.027) (-0.56)			0.566 (0.078)*** (7.17)	-0.035 (0.027) (-1.26)	
N	274	274	251	251	207	207	251	251	488	488	207	207
R^2	0.22	0.51	0.37	0.33	0.23	0.24	0.40	0.31	0.31	0.19	0.22	0.19
F-statistics	11.54	47.68	21.69	24.83	6.84	19.01	29.67	14.54	25.37	25.11	8.28	8.77
F-stat. of joint null	4.58	1.60	11.11	8.77	1.90	8.73	16.50	2.33				

(*) Indicates marginal significance at the 10%-level, (**) at the 5%-level, (***) at the 1%-level. Robust standard errors and t-statistics are reported below the estimated parameters.

Table 3. SEM results using information on PRIVO and MCAP to measure financial development (by subsamples)

Dependent variable: Domestic-to-Total debt and BTOT, Simultaneous equations model

	"High income" group		"Medium income"		"Low income"		"Medium income"		"Medium income"		"Low income"	
	1st eq.	2nd eq,	1st eq.	2nd eq.	1st eq.	2nd eq.	1st eq.	2nd eq.	1st eq.	2nd eq.	1st eq.	2nd eq.
Domestic-to-Total debt		1.826		0.973		0.358		1.515		0.120		0.396
		(0.494)***		(0.213)***		(0.062)***		(0.154)***		(0.010)***		(0.073)***
		(3.69)		(4.56)		(5.76)		(9.83)		(11.39)		(5.41)
PRIVO	-0.114		0.488		0.129		-0.344		-0.542		0.138	
	(0.085)		(0.088)***		(0.057)**		(0.142)***		(0.151)***		(0.034)***	
	(-1.34)		(5.48)		(2.25)		(-2.41)		(-3.58)		(4.03)	
Inflation	-2.367	1.320	-0.054	-0.058	-0.182	0.099	0.002	-0.016	-0.010	-0.002	-0.355	-0.344
	(0.382)***	(1.359)	(0.193)	(0.237)	(0.712)	(0.346)	(0.097)	(0.150)	(0.103)	(0.130)	(0.710)	(0.365)
	(-6.19)	(0.97)	(-0.28)	(-0.25)	(-0.26)	(0.29)	(0.02)	(-0.11)	(-0.10)	(-0.02)	(-0.50)	(-0.94)
MCAP							0.386		0.434			
							(0.067)***		(0.072)***			
							(5.73)		(6.02)			
Total debt/GDP			-0.179		0.196		0.633		0.457		0.171	
			(0.279)		(0.197)		(0.366)*		(0.363)		(0.164)	
			(-0.64)		(0.99)		(1.73)		(1.26)		(1.04)	
Law and Order		0.075		0.013	-0.027				-0.029			
		(0.034)**		(0.014)	(0.009)***				(0.011)***			
		(2.18)		(0.89)	(-2.89)				(-2.58)			
Savings rate	-0.038		0.017		0.038		0.038		0.040		0.042	
	(0.024)		(0.010)		(0.017)**		(0.011)***		(0.011)***		(0.012)***	
	(-1.56)		(1.65)*		(2.17)		(3.45)		(3.48)		(3.26)	
Trade openness		-0.018		0.015		-0.054		0.036		0.032		-0.047
		(0.005)***		(0.003)***		(0.017)***		(0.004)***		(0.003)***		(0.017)***
		(-3.68)		(4.35)		(-3.10)		(8.73)		(8.92)		
Government Stability		0.058		0.017	0.028			-0.007	0.020			0.025
		(0.014)***		(0.010)	(0.060)			(0.102)	(0.007)***			(0.026)
		(3.95)		(1.60)	(0.47)			(-0.07)	(2.77)			(0.97)
Quality of Bureaucracy		0.239		0.032				-0.075	0.117			0.017
		(0.054)***		(0.038)				(0.034)**	(0.020)***			(0.007)**
		(4.42)		(0.84)				(-2.19)	(5.69)			(2.33)
Exchange rate volatility	-0.042		0.097									
	(0.035)		(0.237)									
	(-1.20)		(0.41)									
Risk index (ICRG)	0.062		0.034			0.024	0.087			0.059	-0.023	
	(0.035)*		(0.027)			(0.007)***	(0.207)			(0.023)***	(0.015)	
	(1.77)		(1.25)			(3.20)	(0.42)			(2.55)	(-1.49)	
N	299	299	302	302	186	186	468	468	468	468	186	186
R^2	0.10	0.10	0.39	0.41	0.46	0.44	0.10	-0.23	0.01	0.06	0.44	0.41
F-statistics	10.53	21.76	16.99	28.26	14.41	21.01	21.17	38.13	19.12	61.06	17.19	19.75
F-stat. of joint null	1.34	21.85	2.08	7.88	5.00	7.32	10.91	26.89	12.95	52.97	4.20	3.50

(*) Indicates marginal significance at the 10%-level, (**) at the 5%-level, (***) at the 1%-level. Robust standard errors and t-statistics are reported below the estimated parameters.

Table 4. SEM results using information on constructed indicators to measure financial development (by subsamples)

Dependent variables: Domestic-to-Total debt and FD/FDEPTH, Simultaneous equations model

	"High income" group		"Medium income"		"Low income"		"High income"		"Medium income"		"Medium income"		"Medium income"	
	1st eq.	2nd eq,	1st eq.	2nd eq.	1st eq.	2nd eq.	1st eq.	2nd eq.	1st eq.	2nd eq.	1st eq.	2nd eq.	1st eq.	2nd eq.
Domestic-to-Total debt		-0.143 (0.185) (-0.77)		5.782 (0.654)*** (8.83)		0.621 (0.116)*** (5.35)		0.318 (0.095)*** (3.34)		0.331 (0.058)*** (5.70)		0.710 (0.092)*** (7.71)		5.877 (1.058)*** (5.55)
FD	0.095 (0.016)*** (5.63)		0.038 (0.022)* (1.73)								0.831 (0.178)*** (4.66)		0.044 (0.012)*** (3.60)	
FDEPTH					0.192 (0.257) (0.74)		2.161 (1.002)** (2.16)		0.569 (0.249)** (2.29)					
Inflation	0.468 (0.515) (0.91)	-0.205 (0.035)*** (-5.72)	0.045 (0.093) (0.48)	-0.101 (0.678) (-1.49)	-0.325 (0.827) (-0.39)	-0.284 (0.647) (-0.44)	0.096 (0.157) (0.61)	-0.080 (0.024)*** (-3.25)	0.130 (0.957) (0.14)	-0.010 (0.469) (-0.02)	-0.099 (0.107) (-0.92)	-0.016 (0.005)*** (-2.79)	0.088 (0.095) (0.93)	-0.126 (0.669)* (-1.89)
Total debt/ GDP	-0.724 (0.401)* (-1.80)		0.595 (0.353)* (1.68)		0.888 (1.959) (0.45)		4.638 (7.171) (0.65)		0.432 (0.311) (1.39)		1.010 (0.642) (1.57)		0.315 (0.420) (0.75)	
Law and Order			-0.046 (0.010)*** (-4.38)		-0.238 (0.099)*** (-2.41)				-0.316 (0.090)*** (-3.48)			0.474 (0.084)*** (5.65)		0.454 (0.076)*** (5.93)
Savings rate	-0.051 (0.018)*** (-2.84)		0.053 (0.011)*** (4.72)		0.071 (0.019)*** (3.74)		-0.011 (0.032) (-0.35)		0.019 (0.008)** (2.21)		0.377 (0.198)** (1.90)		0.047 (0.010)*** (4.31)	
Trade openness	0.011 (0.002)*** (5.26)	-0.017 (0.016) (-1.02)	-0.010 (0.003)*** (-2.65)	0.161 (0.017)*** (9.39)	-0.088 (0.041)** (-2.11)	-0.015 (0.032) (-0.48)	0.039 (0.041) (0.96)	-0.011 (0.008) (-1.25)	-0.164 (0.037)*** (-4.36)	0.112 (0.012)*** (8.95)	-0.072 (0.037)** (-1.93)	0.068 (0.021)*** (3.12)		0.166 (0.016)*** (10.01)
Government Stability	-0.037 (0.007)*** (-5.26)		0.013 (0.006)** (1.94)		0.074 (0.069) (1.07)		-0.176 (0.077)** (-2.27)		0.127 (0.061)** (2.09)			0.122 (0.058)** (2.09)		0.067 (0.047) (1.40)
Quality of Bureaucracy			0.086 (0.030)*** (2.85)				-0.796 (0.477)* (-1.67)		0.807 (0.233)*** (3.45)			0.397 (0.179)** (2.22)		0.401 (0.185)** (2.16)
Exchange rate volatility							-0.025 (0.039) (-0.64)				0.031 (0.031) (0.99)			
Risk index (ICRG)		0.129 (0.023)*** (5.54)		0.081 (0.011)*** (6.99)		0.073 (0.013)*** (5.28)		0.029 (0.008)*** (3.53)		0.077 (0.007)*** (10.61)	-0.038 (0.031) (-1.22)		-0.003 (0.002) (-1.17)	
N	297	297	433	433	186	186	288	288	594	594	215	215	433	433
R^2	0.27	0.24	0.38	0.49	0.37	0.49	0.10	0.41	0.20	0.35	0.52	0.67	0.297	0.516
F-statistics	13.42	34.69	18.28	78.39	10.46	31.46	10.99	55.20	12.96	102.48	18.04	71.79	13.38	59.01

(*) Indicates marginal significance at the 10%-level, (**) at the 5%-level, (***) at the 1%-level. Robust standard errors and t-statistics are reported below the estimated parameters.

Table 5. SEM results using information on constructed indicators to measure financial development (by subsamples)

Dependent variable: Domestic-to-Total debt and FDBANK/FDSTOCK/FDEFF/FDSIZE, Simultaneous equations model

	"High income" group		"Medium income"		"Low income"		"High income"		"Medium income"		"High income"		"Medium income"	
	1st eq.	2nd eq.	1st eq.	2nd eq.	1st eq.	2nd eq.	1st eq.	2nd eq.	1st eq.	2nd eq.	1st eq.	2nd eq.	1st eq.	2nd eq.
Domestic-to-Total debt		0.071 (0.131) (0.54)		0.339 (0.054)*** (6.17)		1.023 (0.137)*** (7.45)		-0.208 (0.183) (-1.13)		0.437 (0.072)*** (6.00)		0.213 (0.109)** (1.95)		0.398 (0.063)*** (6.24)
FDBANK	0.398 (0.205)** (1.94)		0.575 (0.233)*** (2.46)		0.403 (0.196)** (2.05)									
FDSTOCK							0.499 (0.218)** (2.28)		0.692 (0.204)*** (3.39)					
FDSIZE											1.532 (0.476)*** (3.21)		1.322 (0.276)*** (4.79)	
Inflation	-0.075 (0.046) (-1.61)	-0.183 (0.031)*** (-5.79)	0.045 (0.095) (0.47)	-0.010 (0.005)** (-2.04)	0.204 (0.106)** (1.92)	-0.323 (0.092)*** (-3.50)	-0.124 (0.040)*** (-3.08)	-0.088 (0.032)*** (-2.72)	-0.295 (0.094)*** (-3.14)	0.089 (0.550) (0.16)	-0.088 (0.571) (-0.15)	-0.066 (0.020)*** (-3.21)	0.013 (0.021) (0.61)	-0.023 (0.008)*** (-2.67)
Total debt/ GDP	1.063 (3.702) (0.29)		2.383 (2.086) (1.14)		-4.172 (3.009) (-1.39)		3.434 4.005 (0.86)		2.294 (0.578)*** (3.97)		0.114 (0.397) (0.29)		0.212 (0.724) (0.29)	
Law and Order		0.383 (0.087)*** (4.38)	-0.388 (0.098)*** (3.94)		-0.317 (0.124)*** (-2.56)					0.302 (0.072)*** (4.15)				0.200 (0.059)*** (3.36)
Savings rate	-0.271 (0.157)* (-1.72)		0.041 (0.009)*** (4.52)		0.020 (0.022) (0.89)		0.234 (0.158) (1.47)		0.682 (0.175)*** (3.88)		-0.019 (0.172) (-0.11)		0.261 (0.199) (1.31)	
Trade openness		0.055 (0.013)*** (4.07)	-0.177 (0.039)*** (-4.49)	0.164 (0.013)*** (12.30)		-0.096 (0.050)** (-1.90)		-0.041 (0.012)*** (-3.32)	-0.042 (0.032) (-1.29)	0.016 (0.019) (0.86)		0.021 (0.008)*** (2.62)	-0.047 (0.039) (-1.18)	0.038 (0.015)*** (2.41)
Government Stability		0.008 (0.042) (0.18)	0.103 (0.061)* (1.68)		-0.039 (0.669) (-0.06)		-0.215 (0.072)*** (-3.00)			0.099 (0.052)* (1.88)	-0.362 (0.086)*** (-4.16)			0.075 (0.040)* (1.84)
Quality of Bureaucracy		0.569 (0.143)*** (3.96)	0.849 (0.225)*** (3.77)							0.292 (0.146)** (2.00)	-0.522 (0.421) (-1.24)			0.379 (0.128)*** (2.95)
Exchange rate volatility									-0.057 (0.029)** (-1.94)				-0.015 (0.033) (-0.46)	
Risk index (ICRG)	0.044 (0.026)*			0.069 (0.008)*** (8.02)		0.083 (0.018)*** (4.50)		0.090 (0.019)*** (4.62)	0.035 (0.281) (0.12)			0.045 (0.012)*** (3.60)	0.014 (0.317) (0.05)	
N	318	318	543	543	155	155	326	326	243	243	311	311	228	228
R^2	0.24	0.48	0.29	0.44	0.48	0.55	0.10	0.04	0.49	0.51	0.19	0.35	0.40	0.54
F-statistics	11.65	44.09	18.54	100.45	11.84	39.72	7.63	15.93	21.56	30.08	9.63	32.21	14.75	46.60

(*) Indicates marginal significance at the 10%-level, (**) at the 5%-level, (***) at the 1%-level. Robust standard errors and t-statistics are reported below the estimated parameters.

APPENDIX V. GMM REGRESSION RESULTS

Table 1. GMM results using information on LLY, BTOT, PRIVO and MCAP to measure financial development (by subsamples)

Dependent variable: "Domestic-to-Total debt"(Y), GMM

	"High income" group 1	"Middle income" group 2	"Low income" group 3	"High income" group 4	"Middle income" group 5	"Low income" group 6	"High income" group 7	"Middle income" group 8	"Low income" group 9	"Middle income" Group 10
L. Y	0.631	0.625	0.506	0.551	0.598	0.4721	0.688	0.691	0.487	0.627
	(0.137)***	(0.107)***	(0.117)	(0.118)***	(0.107)***	(0.117)***	(0.048)***	(0.100)***	(0.144)***	(0.105)***
LLY	-0.093	0.184	-0.032							0.225
	(0.079)	(0.069)***	(0.184)							(0.065)***
BTOT				0.166	0.175	0.181				
				(0.083)**	(0.096)*	(0.086)**				
PRIVO							0.093	0.035	-0.182	
							(0.040)**	(0.044)	(0.438)	
MCAP	0.024	0.042		0.028	0.052		0.047	0.023		0.023
	(0.016)	(0.024)*		(0.021)	(0.025)**		(0.204)	(0.026)		(0.019)
Inflation	-0.056	-0.002	-0.080	-0.066	0.031	0.015	-0.069	-0.004	-0.015	0.040
	(0.053)	(0.040)	(0.094)	(0.062)	(0.033)	(0.020)	(0.054)	(0.004)	(0.009)	(0.044)
Savings rate	-0.046	-0.035	-0.029	-0.027	-0.076	-0.002	0.055	-0.078	0.082	-0.081
	(0.034)	(0.107)	(0.162)	(0.030)	(0.104)	(0.012)	(0.269)	(0.110)	(0.089)	(0.095)
Trade	0.002	0.023	0.029	-0.032	0.029	0.013	-0.059	0.084	0.023	0.012
	(0.037)	(0.061)	(0.045)	(0.037)	(0.046)	(0.566)	(0.092)	(0.059)	(0.040)	(0.057)
Government Stability		0.059		-0.063	0.057			0.047	-0.038	
		(0.021)***		(0.047)	(0.022)***			(0.024)**	(0.040)	
Bq		0.010		0.035	0.012			0.010	-0.013	
		(0.014)		(0.034)	(0.013)			(0.013)	(0.016)	
Real exchange rate	0.003			-0.039						
	(0.017)			(0.207)						
Risk Index	0.046		0.019			0.023	0.049			0.035
	(0.012)***		(0.017)			(0.015)	(0.013)***			(0.010)***
Total debt/GDP	0.345	0.018	0.423	0.114	0.122	0.605	0.161	-0.066	0.477	0.068
	(0.751)	(0.191)	(0.189)**	(0.107)	(0.280)	(0.325)*	(0.122)	(0.178)	(0.299)	(0.213)
N	221	398	149	218	413	167	256	398	149	398
A-bond AR(1): prob>z	0.107	0.001	0.025	0.154	0.003	0.021	0.079	0.001	0.019	0.001
A-bond AR(2): prob>z	0.190	0.5626	0.630	0.130	0.338	0.714	0.102	0.585	0.441	0.309

(*) Indicates marginal significance at the 10%-level, (**) at the 5%-level, (***) at the 1%-level. Robust standard errors are reported below the estimated parameters.

Table 2. GMM results using information on constructed indicators to measure financial development (by subsamples)

Dependent variable: "Domestic-to-Total debt"(Y), GMM

	"High income" group	"Middle income" group	"Low income" group	"High income" group	"Middle income" group	"Low income" group	"High income" group	"Middle income" group	"Low income" group	"Middle income" group
	1	2	3	4	5	6	7	8	9	10
L. Y	0.643	0.586	0.495	0.706	0.595	0.447	0.763	0.579	0.462	0.585
	(0.116)***	(0.095)***	(0.212)**	(0.077)***	(0.090)***	(0.118)***	(0.045)***	(0.094)***	(0.120)***	(096)***
FD	-0.079	0.022	0.034							0.025
	(0.089)	(0.008)***	(0.020)*							(0.007)***
FDEPTH				0.022	0.039	0.011	0.049	0.041	0.019	
				(0.008)***	(0.015)***	(0.019)	(0.025)**	(0.018)**	(0.018)	
Inflation	-0.068	-0.016	0.001	-0.029	0.099	-0.063	-0.025	0.009	-0.010	-0.128
	(0.036)*	(0.383)	(0.171)	(0.030)	(0.041)**	(0.089)	(0.031)	(0.263)	(0.009)	(0.380)
Savings rate	-0.028	-0.022	-0.022	-0.018	-0.020	0.066	0.010	-0.022	0.011	-0.014
	(0.027)	(0.010)**	(0.043)	(0.029)	(0.011)*	(0.134)	(0.029)	(0.158)	(0.011)	(0.011)
Trade	-0.027	0.078	0.044	-0.005	0.057	-0.006	-0.068	0.052	-0.025	0.080
	(0.039)	(0.037)**	(0.099)	(0.050)	(0.057)	(0.054)	(0.082)	(0.061)	(0.053)	(0.038)**
Government Stability				-0.042				0.010	-0.058	0.028
				(0.034)				(0.026)	(0.034)*	(0.025)
Bq				0.044				0.012	-0.015	0.004
				(0.034)				(0.011)	(0.020)	(0.010)
Real exchange rate	0.002			0.002	0.014*			0.028		
	(0.169)			(0.016)	(0.083)			(0.088)		
Risk Index	0.041	0.032	-0.014		0.063	0.016	0.051			
	(0.017)**	(0.012)***	(0.027)		(0.010)***	(0.017)	(0.017)***			
Total debt/GDP	0.037	-0.144	-0.093	0.150	0.101	0.435	0.167	0.521	0.470	-0.242
	(0.136)	(0.166)	(0.855)	(0.118)	(0.051)**	(0.184)***	(0.116)	(0.437)	(0.187)***	(0.127)**
N	208	362	62	226	257	149	256	257	149	362
A-bond AR(1): prob>z	0.154	0.003	0.045	0.202	0.002	0.030	0.081	0.005	0.027	0.002
A-bond AR(2): prob>z	0.241	0.860	0.592	0.187	0.918	0.588	0.122	0.255	0.459	0.819

Notes: Specification choice, Original GMM.

(i) Domestic debt regressors are lagged one period, (ii) original GMM results obtained using STATA's xtabond command, (iii) Arellano-bond AR(1) and AR(2) tests are for 1st and 2nd –order serial correlation in errors. 1st order serial correlation is expected; model identification requires absence of 2nd order correlation, (iv))GMM instrumentation: Financial development indicators are treated as endogenous, "law and order" is used as excluded instruments. Instruments used for differenced equation: X_{t-2}, where X denotes endogenous variable.

(*) Indicates marginal significance at the 10%-level, (**) at the 5%-level, (***) at the 1%-level. Robust standard errors are reported below the estimated parameters.

Table 3. GMM results using information on constructed indicators to measure financial development (by subsamples)

Dependent variable: "Domestic-to-Total debt"(Y), GMM

	"High income" group 1	"Middle income" Group 2	"Low income" group 3	"High income" group 4	"Middle income" group 5	"Low income" group 6	"Middle income" group 7	"Middle income" group 8	"Middle income" group 9	"Middle income" Group 10
L. Y	0.669	0.625	0.438	0.603	0.595	0.327	0.635	0.604	0.652	0.636
	(0.095)***	(0.090)***	(0.145)***	(0.147)***	(0.073)***	(0.186)*	(0.089)***	(0.084)***	(0.083)***	(0.084)***
FDBANK	-0.079	0.022	0.039		0.016					
	(0.071)	(0.008)***	(0.287)		(0.009)*					
FDSTOCK							-0.058			
							(0.071)			
FDEFF				-0.013				0.015		
				(0.147)				(0.006)**		
FDSIZE						0.109			0.038	0.037
						(0.039)***			(0.012)***	(0.012)***
Inflation	-0.052	0.021	-0.079	-0.064	0.094	-0.002	-0.077	-0.047	0.012	0.016
	(0.035)	(0.020)	(0.094)	(0.062)	(0.022)***	(0.183)	(0.044)*	(0.047)	(0.005)**	(0.005)***
Savings rate	-0.035	-0.072	-0.011	-0.048	-0.014	-0.028	-0.010	-0.021	-0.018	-0.024
	(0.032)	(0.110)	(0.019)	(0.034)	(0.011)	(0.034)	(0.011)	(0.088)	(0.008)**	(0.007)***
Trade	-0.016	0.073	0.017	-0.024	0.046	0.045	0.013	0.074	0.036	0.035
	(0.041)	(0.043)*	(0.082)	(0.045)	(0.055)	(0.073)	(0.005)***	(0.042)*	(0.045)	(0.047)
Government Stability		0.029	-0.029				0.041	0.039	0.044	
		(0.021)	(0.043)				(0.027	(0.030)	(0.021)**	
Bq		0.039	-0.007				0.010	0.016	0.016	
		(0.084)	(0.158)				(0.010)	(0.010)	(0.011)	
Real exchange rate	0.073			-0.014	0.012					
	(0.167)			(0.023)	(0.009)					
Risk Index	0.026			0.051	0.050	-0.003				0.034
	(0.013)**			(0.015)***	(0.013)***	(0.002)				(0.010)***
Total debt/GDP	0.094	0.033	0.573	0.487	-0.038	0.192	-0.330	-0.247	-0.019	0.094
	(0.120)	(0.160)	(0.670)	(0.979)	(0.390)	(0.834)	(0.137)***	(0.167)	(0.195)	(0.258)
N	221	459	122	231	237	66	414	409	398	398
A-bond AR(1): prob>z	0.178	0.001	0.024	0.077	0.011	0.026	0.002	0.005	0.001	0.001
A-bond AR(2): prob>z	0.251	0.258	0.608	0.2429	0.218	0.795	0.203	0.226	0.563	0.312

(*) Indicates marginal significance at the 10%-level, (**) at the 5%-level, (***) at the 1%-level. Robust standard errors are reported below the estimated parameters.

Table 4. GMM results using information on LLY and MCAP to measure financial development (by subsamples)

Dependent variable: "Domestic-to-Total debt"(Y), GMM 2-step

	"High income" group	"Middle income" group	"Low income" group	"High income" group	"Middle income" group	"Low income" group	"High income" group	"Middle income" group	"Low income" group	"Middle income" group
	1	2	3	4	5	6	7	8	9	10
L. Y	0.568	0.650	0.657	0.691	0.082	0.561	0.780	0.788	0.637	0.666
	(0.288)**	(0.14)***	(0.122)***	(0.112)***	(0.010)***	(0.136)***	(0.158)***	(0.109)***	(0.198)***	(0.124)***
LLY	-0.140	0.157	0.384							0.209
	(0.100)	(0.088)*	(0.139)***							(0.081)***
PRIVO				0.069	0.088	-0.117				
				(0.038)*	(0.052)*	(0.083)				
BTOT							0.185	0.070	0.103	
							(0.070)***	(0.130)	(0.135)	
MCAP	0.035	0.032		0.008	0.051		0.015	0.012		0.017
	(0.013)***	(0.018)*		(0.021)	(0.198)		(0.017)	(0.017)		(0.021)
Inflation	-0.079	-0.043	0.038	-0.070	-0.020	-0.010	-0.001	0.008	0.011	-0.000
	(0.044)*	(0.041)	(0.041)	(0.037)*	(0.034)	(0.007)	(0.315)	(0.026)	(0.032)	(0.000)
Trade	-0.063	0.026	-0.011	-0.011	0.033	0.010	0.020	0.049	0.015	0.013
	(0.035)*	(0.056)	(0.016)	(0.005)*	(0.049)	(0.005)**	(0.010)*	(0.040)	(0.078)	(0.059)
Savings rate	-0.012	0.066	0.025	0.031	-0.087	0.008	-0.004	0.010	0.002	-0.021
	(0.026)	(0.090)	(0.000)	(0.025)	(0.092)	(0.011)	(0.014)	(0.007)	(0.129)	(0.104)
Government	-0.091	0.071					-0.049			
Stability	(0.047)*	(0.019)***					(0.040)			
Bq	0.034	0.011					0.010			
	(0.035)	(0.017)					(0.203)			
Risk Index			0.008	0.066	0.027	0.001		0.025	0.027	0.022
			(0.006)	(0.018)***	(0.009)***	(0.001)		(0.010)**	(0.163)	(0.010)**
Real exchange rate	-0.016									
	(0.021)									
Total debt/GDP	0.021	-0.055	-0.079	0.187	0.051	0.143	-0.095	0.014	0.501	0.005
	(0.185)	(0.124)	(0.160)	(0.103)*	(0.184)	(0.109)	(0.257)	(0.200)	(0.634)	(0.148)
N	221	398	169	256	398	149	286	413	167	398
Hansen's χ^2: prob> χ^2	1.000	1.000	1.000	1.000	1.000	1.000	1.000	1.000	1.000	1.000
A-bond AR(1): prob>z	0.343	0.006	0.039	0.085	0.002	0.089	0.108	0.006	0.087	0.004
A-bond AR(2): prob>z	0.230	0.569	0.611	0.104	0.381	0.520	0.111	0.255	0.696	0.408

(*) Indicates marginal significance at the 10%-level, (**) at the 5%-level, (***) at the 1%-level. Corrected standard errors are reported below the estimated parameters.

Table 5. GMM results using information on constructed indicators to measure financial development (by subsamples)

Dependent variable: "Domestic-to-Total debt"(Y), GMM 2-step

	"High income" group	"Middle income" Group	"Low income" group	"High income" group	"Middle income" Group	"Low income" group	"High income" group	"Middle income" group	"High income" group
	1	2	3	4	5	6	7	8	9
L. Y	0.615	0.827	0.709	0.726	0.421	0.680	0.800	0.406	0.620
	(0.091)***	(0.089)***	(0.220)***	(0.092)***	(0.124)***	(0.211)***	(0.090)***	(0.148)***	(0.165)***
FD	0.035	0.017							
	(0.022)	(0.009)*							
FDEPTH			0.014	0.075	-0.009				0.071
			(0.037)	(0.027)***	(0.014)				(0.015)***
FDBANK						0.012	0.032	0.010	
						(0.247)	(0.032)	(0.016)	
Inflation	-0.043	0.003	0.003	-0.014	-0.005	0.016	-0.032	-0.010	-0.025
	(0.036)	(0.036)	(0.010)	(0.027)	(0.004)	(0.013)	(0.027)	(0.052)	(0.036)
Trade	-0.012	-0.045	-0.002	-0.015	0.015	-0.003	-0.013	0.015	-0.012
	(0.008)	(0.022)**	(0.008)	(0.006)**	(0.007)**	(0.005)	(0.007)*	(0.007)**	(0.005)**
Savings rate	0.043	0.011	0.015	0.047	-0.009	0.020	0.029	-0.008	0.031
	(0.033)	(0.005)*	(0.037)	(0.024)**	(0.011)	(0.018)	(0.026)	(0.010)	(0.023)
Government Stability									-0.009
									(0.002)***
Bq									0.056
									(0.030)*
Real exchange rate									-0.042
									(0.024)*
Risk Index	0.072	0.013	0.061	0.056	0.033	0.016	0.052	0.026	
	(0.021)***	(0.005)**	(0.079)	(0.019)***	(0.010)***	(0.008)*	(0.017)***	(0.011)**	
Total debt/GDP	0.212	0.109	0.307	0.204	0.122	-0.415	0.115	0.214	0.175
	(0.127)	(0.226)	(0.496)	(0.873)**	(0.260)	(0.401)	(0.120)	(0.340)	(0.081)**
N	238	409	169	256	501	143	251	459	226
Hansen's χ^2: prob> χ^2	1.000	1.000	1.000	1.000	0.999	1.000	1.000	0.999	1.000
A-bond AR(1): prob>z	0.088	0.003	0.077	0.097	0.014	0.107	0.082	0.039	0.228
A-bond AR(2): prob>z	0.117	0.966	0.628	0.141	1.000	0.653	0.111	0.445	0.247

(*) Indicates marginal significance at the 10%-level, (**) at the 5%-level, (***) at the 1%-level. Corrected standard errors are reported below the estimated parameters.

Table 6. GMM results using information on constructed indicators to measure financial development (by subsamples)

Dependent variable: "Domestic-to-Total debt"(Y), GMM 2-step

	"High income" group 1	"High income" group 2	"Middle income" group 3	"Low income" group 4	"High income" group 5	"High income" group 6	"Middle income" group 7	"High income" group 8	"Middle income" Group 9
L. Y	0.605	0.628	0.889	0.106	0.675	0.666	0.819	0.671	0.858
	(0.113)***	(0.130)***	(0.057)***	(0.919)	(0.154)***	(0.119)***	(0.060)***	(0.086)***	(0.062)***
FDSTOCK	0.066	0.080	0.015	0.022					
	(0.083)	(0.098)	(0.079)	(0.062)					
FDEFF					0.029	0.031	0.040		
					(0.011)***	(0.018)	(0.080)		
FDSIZE								0.033	0.017
								(0.0252)	(0.012)
Inflation	-0.075	-0.077	-0.047	0.013	-0.064	-0.061	-0.046	-0.051	-0.017
	(0.032)**	(0.038)**	(0.024)*	(0.020)	(0.045)	(0.025)**	(0..029)	(0.032)	(0.068)
Trade	-0.097	-0.012	-0.025	0.002	-0.011	-0.012	-0.022	-0.014	-0.037
	(0.063)	(0.006)*	(0.012)**	(0.000)	(0.007)	(0.006)*	(0.016)	(0.006)**	(0.016)**
Savings rate	0.019	0.032	0.060	-0.049	0.042	0.022	0.096	0.037	0.063
	(0.026)	(0.024)	(0.042)	(0.052)	(0.022)*	(0.022)	(0.034)***	(0.022)	(0.038)
Government		-0.091	0.043		-0.091		0.048		
Stability		(0.049)*	(0.015)***		(0.047)*		(0.020)**		
Bq		-0.029	0.020		-0.044		0.021		
		(0.047)	(0.010)**		(0.499)		(0.011)*		
Risk Index	0.062			0.004		0.068		0.054	0.013
	(0.016)***			(0.005)		(0.017)***		(0.017)***	(0.004)***
Total debt/GDP	0.735	-0.027	-0.178	-0.470	0.076	0.164	0.013	0.147	-0.057
	(0.808)	(0.113)	(0.211)	(0.172)**	(0.107)	(0.137)	(0.225)	(0.093)	(0.097)
N	266	266	462	82	261	261	459	251	440
Hansen's χ^2: prob> χ^2	1.000	1.000	1.000	1.000	1.000	1.000	1.000	1.000	1.000
A-bond AR(1): prob>z	0.090	0.076	0.003	0.207	0.085	0.074	0.004	0.084	0.001
A-bond AR(2): prob>z	0.109	0.125	0.196	0.987	0.108	0.116	0.269	0.106	0.441

Notes: Specification choice: 2-step GMM.

(i) Domestic debt regressors are lagged one period, (ii) 2-step GMM results obtained using STATA's xtabond2 command, (iii) Arellano-bond AR(1) and AR(2) tests are for 1st and 2nd –order serial correlation in errors. 1st order serial correlation is expected; model identification requires absence of 2nd order correlation, (iv) Hansen's chi squared test checks if the moment conditions used by the system GMM estimator are valid, (v) Windmeijer-corrected cluster-robust errors are reported below the estimated parameters, (vi) Orthogonal deviations are used to maximize sample size, (vii))GMM instrumentation: Financial development indicators are treated as endogenous, "law and order" is used as excluded instruments (iv-style instruments). Instruments used for the orthogonal deviations equation: X_{t-2}, where X denotes endogenous variable.

(*) indicates marginal significance at the 10%-level, (**) at the 5%-level, (***) at the 1%-level. Corrected standard errors are reported below the estimated parameters.

APPENDIX VI. PROOFS OF RESULTS IN THE MAIN TEXT

a) Case $\phi = 1$ (ϕ stands for the share of nominal bonds in total banks' debtholding).

The government maximizes the following objective function with respect to π:

$$\max_{\pi} C = Y - \frac{1}{2}\mu\pi^2 - \lambda T \quad (6.1)$$

subject to

$$c_2 \leq \omega_1 + (1 + r^*)\mathrm{b}_\mathrm{j}^* + (1 + r_b - \gamma\pi)b_j + (1 + r_d - \gamma\pi)d_{j0} - T$$
$$c_2 \geq 0$$

where $T = \beta(1 + r - \gamma\pi)b_b + (1 - \beta)(1 + r^*)b_s^* + (1 + r^*)b_f^*$ (6.2)

Total deposits raised by banks at t=0 to purchase the public bonds: $d_{total} = (1 - \beta)(\omega_0 - b_s^*)$

Deposits raised by 1 bank: $d_{1bank} = \frac{1-\beta}{\beta}(\omega_0 - b_s^*)$

Investment of 1 bank in public bonds at $t = 0$: $b_b = \omega_0 + \frac{1-\beta}{\beta}(\omega_0 - b_s^*)$

The wealth of Banks in $t = 1$ is given by:

$$W_{1b} = \omega_{1b} + (1 + r - \gamma\pi)[\omega_0 + \frac{1 - \beta}{\beta}(\omega_0 - b_s^*)] -$$
$$-(1 + r - \gamma\pi)\frac{1 - \beta}{\beta}(\omega_0 - b_s^*) - T =$$

$$= \omega_{1b} + (1 + r - \gamma\pi)\omega_0 - \beta(1 + r - \gamma\pi)b_b - (1 - \beta)(1 + r^*)\mathrm{b}_\mathrm{s}^* -$$
$$-(1 + \mathrm{r}^*)\mathrm{b}_\mathrm{f}^* = \omega_{1b} + (1 + r - \gamma\pi)\omega_0 - \beta(1 + r - \gamma\pi)\omega_0 -$$
$$-(1 + r - \gamma\pi)(1 - \beta)(\omega_0 - b_s^*) -$$
$$-(1 - \beta)(1 + r^*)\mathrm{b}_\mathrm{s}^* - (1 + \mathrm{r}^*)\mathrm{b}_\mathrm{f}^* \rightarrow$$
$$W_{1b} = \omega_{1b} + (1 - \beta)b_s^*(r - r^* - \gamma\pi) - (1 + r^*)\mathrm{b}_\mathrm{f}^* \tag{6.3}$$

consequently, banks wealth is decreasing in π.

The wealth of savers in t=1 is given by:

$$W_{1s} = \omega_{1s} + (1 + r^*)b_s^* + (1 + r - \gamma\pi)(\omega_0 - b_s^*) - T =$$
$$= \omega_{1s} + (1 + r^*)b_s^* + (1 + r - \gamma\pi)(\omega_0 - b_s^*) -$$
$$-\beta(1 + r - \gamma\pi)b_b - (1 - \beta)(1 + r^*)b_s^* - (1 + r^*)b_f^* =$$
$$= \omega_{1s} + (1 + r^*)b_s^* +$$
$$+ (1 + r - \gamma\pi)(\omega_0 - b_s^*) - \beta(1 + r - \gamma\pi)[\omega_0 + \frac{1 - \beta}{\beta}(\omega_0 - b_s^*)] -$$
$$- (1 - \beta)(1 + r^*)b_s^* - (1 + r^*)b_f^*$$
$$W_{1s} = \omega_{1b} - \beta b_s^*(r - r^* - \gamma\pi) - (1 + r^*)\mathrm{b}_\mathrm{f}^* \tag{6.4}$$

Hence, savers wealth is increasing in π.

Applying $Y = \beta W_{1b} + (1 - \beta)W_{1s} + \frac{A_H - (1+r^*)}{(1+r^*) - \alpha A_H}\beta W_b$, we get

$$Y = \beta\omega_{1b} + \beta(1 - \beta)b_s^*(r - r^* - \gamma\pi) + (1 - \beta)\omega_{1s} -$$
$$-\beta(1 - \beta)b_s^*(r - r^* - \gamma\pi) - (1 + r^*)b_f^* +$$
$$+\frac{A_H - (1 + r^*)}{(1 + r^*) - \alpha A_H}\beta W_b = \beta\omega_{1b} + (1 - \beta)\omega_{1s} - (1 + r^*)b_f^* +$$
$$+\frac{A_H - (1+r^*)}{(1+r^*) - \alpha A_H}\beta W_b \rightarrow$$
$$Y = W_1 + \frac{A_H - (1+r^*)}{(1+r^*) - \alpha A_H}\beta\left[\omega_{1b} + (1 - \beta)b_s^*(r - r^* - \gamma\pi) - (1 + r^*)b_f^*\right] -$$
$$-(1 + r^*)b_f^* \tag{6.5}$$

The first-order condition of maximization problem implies

$$\frac{\partial C}{\partial \pi} = \frac{\partial y}{\partial \pi} - \mu\pi - \lambda\frac{\partial T}{\partial \pi} = -\frac{A_H - (1+r^*)}{(1+r^*) - \alpha A_H}\beta(1 - \beta)b_s^*\gamma - \mu\pi + \lambda\beta\gamma b_b =$$
$$= -\frac{A_H - (1+r^*)}{(1+r^*) - \alpha A_H}\beta(1 - \beta)b_s^*\gamma - \mu\pi + \lambda\beta\gamma[\omega_0 + \frac{(1-\beta)}{\beta}(\omega_0 - b_s^*)] \geq 0$$

Equilibrium Inflation in low productivity state satisfies

$$\pi^L = \frac{1}{\mu}\lambda\beta\gamma[\omega_0 + \frac{1-\beta}{\beta}(\omega_0 - b_s^*)] = \frac{1}{\mu}\lambda\gamma[\omega_0 - b_s^* + \beta b_s^*] \rightarrow$$
$$\pi^L = \frac{1}{\mu}\lambda\gamma[\omega_0 - (1-\beta)b_s^*] \quad (6.6)$$

While, inflation in high productivity state satisfies

$$\pi^H = \frac{1}{\mu}\lambda\beta\gamma[\omega_0 + \frac{1-\beta}{\beta}(\omega_0 - b_s^*)] - \frac{1}{\mu}\frac{A_H - (1+r^*)}{(1+r^*) - \alpha A_H}\beta(1-\beta)\gamma b_s^* =$$
$$= \frac{1}{\mu}\lambda\gamma[\omega_0 - b_s^* + \beta b_s^*] - \frac{1}{\mu}\frac{A_H - (1+r^*)}{(1+r^*) - \alpha A_H}\beta(1-\beta)\gamma b_s^* \rightarrow$$
$$\pi^H = \frac{1}{\mu}\lambda\gamma[\omega_0 - (1-\beta)b_s^*] - \frac{1}{\mu}\frac{A_H - (1+r^*)}{(1+r^*) - \alpha A_H}\beta(1-\beta)\gamma b_s^* = \pi^L -$$
$$-\frac{1}{\mu}\frac{A_H - (1+r^*)}{(1+r^*) - \alpha A_H}\beta(1-\beta)\gamma b_s^* \quad (6.7)$$

Expected inflation can be defined as

$$\mathbb{E}\pi = p\pi^H + (1-p)\pi^L = p[\pi^L - \frac{\gamma}{\mu}\vartheta\beta(1-\beta)b_s^*] + (1-p)\pi^L =$$
$$= \frac{\gamma}{\mu}\lambda[\omega_0 - (1-\beta)b_s^*] - p\frac{\gamma}{\mu}\vartheta\beta(1-\beta)b_s^*$$

The nominal interest rate on domestic public bonds, r, defined implicitly yields:

By applying Fisher equation $p(1 + r - \gamma\pi^H) + (1-p)(1 + r - \gamma\pi^L) = = 1 + r^*$, we get

$$p(1 + r + \frac{\gamma}{\mu}\left(\frac{A_H - (1+r^*)}{(1+r^*) - \alpha A_H}\beta(1-\beta)b_s^*\gamma - \lambda\gamma[\omega_0 - (1-\beta)b_s^*]\right)$$
$$+ (1-p)(1 + r - \frac{\gamma}{\mu}\lambda\gamma[\omega_0 -$$
$$-(1-\beta)b_s^*]) = 1 + r^*$$
$$p(1+r) + \frac{P}{\mu}\gamma^2\left(\frac{A_H - (1+r^*)}{(1+r^*) - \alpha A_H}\beta(1-\beta)b_s^* - \lambda[\omega_0 - (1-\beta)b_s^*]\right)$$
$$+ (1-p)(1+r) -$$
$$-\frac{\lambda}{\mu}\gamma^2[\omega_0 - (1-\beta)b_s^*] + \frac{P}{\mu}\lambda\gamma^2[\omega_0 - (1-\beta)b_s^*] = 1 + r^* \rightarrow$$
$$r = r^* + \frac{\lambda}{\mu}\gamma^2[\omega_0 - (1-\beta)b_s^*)] - \frac{P}{\mu}\frac{A_H - (1+r^*)}{(1+r^*) - \alpha A_H}\beta(1-\beta)b_s^*\gamma^2 \quad (6.8)$$

Expected total output of the economy can be defined as

$$\mathbb{E}Y = pY^H + (1-p)Y^L$$

where

$$Y^H = W_1 + \frac{A_H - (1+r^*)}{(1+r^*) - \alpha A_H}\beta\big[\omega_{1b} + (1-\beta)b_s^*(r - r^* - \gamma\pi^H) -$$
$$-(1+r^*)b_f^*\big] - (1+r^*)b_f^* \qquad (6.9)$$

and, $Y^L = W_1 - (1+r^*)b_f^*$ (6.10)

By using the expressions for π from equation (6.7), for r from equation (6.8) and for Y^H and Y^L from equations (6.9) and (6.10) respectively, we can define expected total output of the economy as

$$\mathbb{E}Y = p[W_1 + \frac{A_H - (1+r^*)}{(1+r^*) - \alpha A_H}\beta\big[\omega_{1b} + (1-\beta)b_s^*(r - r^* - \gamma\pi^H) - (1+$$
$$+r^*)b_f^*\big] - (1+r^*)b_f^*] + (1-p)\big[W_1 - (1+r^*)b_f^*\big] =$$
$$= W_1 - (1+r^*)b_f^* + p\frac{A_H - (1+r^*)}{(1+r^*) - \alpha A_H}\beta[\omega_{1b} +$$
$$+(1-\beta)b_s^*(r - r^* - \gamma\pi^H) - (1+r^*)b_f^*] = W_1 - (1+r^*)b_f^* +$$
$$+p\vartheta\beta[\omega_{1b} + (1-\beta)b_s^*(1-\mathrm{p})\frac{1}{\mu}\gamma^2\vartheta\beta(1-\beta)b_s^* - (1+r^*)b_f^*] =$$
$$= W_1 - (1+r^*)b_f^*(1+p\vartheta\beta) + p\vartheta\beta[\omega_{1b} + (1-p)\frac{1}{\mu}\gamma^2\vartheta\beta(1-\beta)^2 b_s^{*2}] \rightarrow$$
$$\mathbb{E}Y = W_1 - (1+r^*)b_f^*(1+p\vartheta\beta) + p\vartheta\beta\omega_{1b} + \underbrace{\frac{\gamma^2 p(1-p)\beta^2\Theta^2(1-\beta)^2 b_s^{*2}}{\mu}}_{Gain\ from\ having\ nominal\ debt} \qquad (6.11)$$

where we have defined as $\vartheta = \frac{A_H - (1+r^*)}{(1+r^*) - \alpha A_H}$ (6.12) and, we have considered $(1-\beta)b_s^*(r - r^* - \gamma\pi^H) = (1-\beta)b_s^*(1-\mathrm{p})\frac{1}{\mu}\gamma^2\vartheta\beta(1-\beta)b_s^*$.

b) Case $0 < \phi < 1$ (ϕ stands for the share of nominal bonds in total banks' debtholding)

The government maximizes the following objective function with respect to π:

$$\max_{\pi} C = Y - \frac{1}{2}\mu\pi^2 - \lambda T \qquad (6.13)$$

where

$$T = \phi\beta(1 + r - \gamma\pi)b_b + (1 - \phi)\beta(1 + r^*)b_b + (1 - \beta)(1 + r^*)b_s^* + +(1 + r^*)b_f^* \qquad (6.14)$$

$$Y^{\psi} = \beta W_{1b} + (1 - \beta)W_{1s} + \frac{A_H - (1+r^*)}{(1+r^*) - \alpha A_H}\beta W_b \qquad (6.15)$$

The wealth of Banks in $t = 1$ is given by

$$W_{1b} = \omega_{1b} + (1 + r - \gamma\pi)\phi[\omega_0 + \frac{1-\beta}{\beta}(\omega_0 - b_s^*)] - -(1 + r - \gamma\pi)\frac{1-\beta}{\beta}(\omega_0 - b_s^*) + + (1 + r^*)(1 - \phi)[\omega_0 + \frac{1-\beta}{\beta}(\omega_0 - b_s^*)] - T = \omega_{1b} + (1 + r - -\gamma\pi)\phi[\omega_0 + \frac{1-\beta}{\beta}(\omega_0 - b_s^*)] - - (1 + r - \gamma\pi)\frac{1-\beta}{\beta}(\omega_0 - b_s^*) + (1 + r^*)(1 - \phi)[\omega_0 + \frac{1-\beta}{\beta}(\omega_0 - -b_s^*)] - \phi\beta(1 + r - \gamma\pi)b_b - (1 - \phi)\beta(1 + r^*)b_b - (1 - \beta)(1 + r^*)b_s^* - -(1 + r^*)b_f^* \rightarrow$$

$$W_{1b} = \omega_{1b} + (r - r^* - \gamma\pi)\frac{1-\beta}{\beta}[\underbrace{\phi(\omega_0 - (1 - \beta)b_s^*)}_{nominal\ bonds} - \underbrace{(\omega_0 - b_s^*)]}_{deposits\ in\ domestic\ currency} - (1 + r^*)b_f^* \qquad (6.16)$$

The wealth of Savers in $t = 1$ is given by

$$W_{1s} = \omega_{1s} + (1 + r^*)b_s^* + (1 + r - \gamma\pi)(\omega_0 - b_s^*) - T = = \omega_{1s} + (1 + r^*)b_s^* + (1 + r - \gamma\pi)(\omega_0 - b_s^*) - - \phi\beta(1 + r - \gamma\pi)b_b - (1 - \phi)\beta(1 + r^*)b_b - (1 - \beta)(1 + r^*)b_s^* - -(1 + r^*)b_f^* \rightarrow$$

$$W_{1s} = \omega_{1s} - (r - r^* - \gamma\pi)\,[\underbrace{\phi(\omega_0 - (1 - \beta)b_s^*)}_{nominal\ bonds\ of\ banks} - \underbrace{(\omega_0 - b_s^*)]}_{deposits\ in\ domestic\ currency} - (1 + r^*)b_f^* \qquad (6.17)$$

Note that there are no aggregate effects from inflation as

$$\beta W_{1b} + (1-\beta)W_{1s} = \beta\omega_{1b} + (1-\beta)\omega_{1s} - (1+r^*)b_f^* = W_1 - \\ -(1+r^*)b_f^*.$$

By using the definition of total output from equation (6.15), we can define output in low and high productivity states respectively:

$$Y^H = \beta W_{1b} + (1-\beta)W_{1s} + \frac{A_H - (1+r^*)}{(1+r^*) - \alpha A_H}\beta W_b = \\ = W_1 + \vartheta\beta\omega_{1b} + (r - r^* - \gamma\pi)\vartheta(1-\beta)[\phi(\omega_0 - \\ -(1-\beta)\mathrm{b}_\mathrm{s}^*) - (\omega_0 - \mathrm{b}_\mathrm{s}^*)] - \vartheta(1+r^*)\beta\mathrm{b}_\mathrm{f}^* - (1+r^*)b_f^* \quad (6.18)$$

where $\vartheta = \frac{A_H - (1+r^*)}{(1+r^*) - \alpha A_H}$, and

$$Y^L = \beta W_{1b} + (1-\beta)W_{1s} = W_1 - (1+r^*)b_f^* \quad (6.19)$$

Expected output of the economy can be expressed in the form of

$$\mathbb{E}Y = pY^H + (1-p)Y^L = \mathrm{p}[W_1 + \vartheta\beta\omega_{1b} + (r - r^* - \gamma\pi^H)\vartheta(1- \\ -\beta)[\phi(\omega_0 - (1-\beta)\mathrm{b}_\mathrm{s}^*) - (\omega_0 - \mathrm{b}_\mathrm{s}^*)] - -\vartheta(1+r^*)\beta\mathrm{b}_\mathrm{f}^* - (1+ \\ +r^*)b_f^*] + (1-p)[W_1 - (1+r^*)b_f^*] = W_1 + p[\vartheta\beta\omega_{1b} + (r - r^* - \\ -\gamma\pi^H)\vartheta(1- -\beta)[\phi(\omega_0 - (1-\beta)b_s^*) - (\omega_0 - b_s^*)] - \vartheta(1+ \\ +r^*)\beta b_f^*] - (1+r^*)b_f^* \quad (6.20)$$

Taxes paid by domestic residents can be written as

$$T = \phi\beta(1 + r - \gamma\pi)b_b + (1-\phi)\beta(1+r^*)b_b + (1-\beta)(1+r^*)b_s^* + \\ + (1+r^*)b_f^* = \\ = (r - r^* - \gamma\pi)\phi[\omega_0 - (1-\beta)b_s^*] + (1+r^*)\omega_0 + (1+r^*)b_f^* \quad (6.21)$$

where $\phi[\omega_0 - (1-\beta)b_s^*]$ is banks' nominal domestic bonds.

$$\mathbb{E}T = p\big[\phi\beta(1 + r - \gamma\pi^H)b_b + (1-\phi)\beta(1+r^*)b_b + (1-\beta)(1+r^*)b_s^{*+} \\ + (1+r^*)b_f^*\big] + \\ +(1-p)[\phi\beta(1 + r - \gamma\pi^L)b_b + (1-\phi)\beta(1+r^*)b_b + (1-\beta)(1+ \\ + r^*)b_s^* + (1+r^*)b_f^*] = (1-\beta)(1+r^*)b_s^* +$$

$$+(1+r^*)b_f^* + (1-\phi)\beta(1+r^*)b_b + \phi\beta(1+r)b_b -$$
$$-\phi\beta\gamma[p\pi^H(1-p)\pi^L]b_b =$$
$$= (1-\beta)(1+r^*)b_s^* + (1+r^*)b_f^* + (1-\phi)\beta(1+r^*)b_{b+}$$
$$+\ \phi\beta(1+r-\gamma\mathbb{E}\pi)b_b = (1-\beta)(1+r^*)b_s^* +$$
$$+(1+r^*)b_f^* + (1-\phi)\beta(1+r^*)b_b + \phi\beta(1+r^*)b_b =$$
$$= (1-\beta)(1+r^*)b_s^* + (1+r^*)b_f^* + \beta(1+r^*)b_b = (1-\beta)(1+r^*)b_s^* +$$
$$+(1+r^*)b_f^* + \beta(1+r^*)\omega_0 + (1-\beta)(1+r^*)(\omega_0 - b_s^*) \rightarrow$$
$$\mathbb{E}T = (1+r^*)b_f^* + (1+r^*)\omega_0 \tag{6.22}$$

The first-order conditions of maximization problem with respect of π implies

$$\frac{\partial C}{\partial \pi^L} = \frac{\partial y^L}{\partial \pi^L} - \mu\pi^L - \lambda\frac{\partial T}{\partial \pi^L} = 0 - \mu\pi^L + \lambda\gamma\phi[\omega_0 - (1-\beta)b_s^*] \geq 0 \rightarrow$$
$$\pi^L = \frac{\gamma}{\mu}\lambda\phi[\omega_0 - (1-\beta)b_s^*] \tag{6.23}$$
$$\frac{\partial C}{\partial \pi^H} = \frac{\partial y^H}{\partial \pi^H} - \mu\pi^H - \lambda\frac{\partial T}{\partial \pi^H} = -\vartheta\gamma(1-\beta)[\phi[\ \omega_0 - (1-\beta)b_s^*] - (\omega_0 -$$
$$-b_s^*)] - \mu\pi^H +$$
$$+\ \lambda\gamma\phi[\omega_0 - (1-\beta)b_s^*] \geq 0 \rightarrow$$

$$\pi^H = \frac{\gamma}{\mu}\lambda\phi[\omega_0 - (1-\beta)b_s^*] -$$
$$-\frac{\gamma}{\mu}\vartheta(1-\beta)[\phi[\omega_0 - (1-\beta)b_s^*] - (\omega_0 - b_s^*)] =$$
$$= \pi^L - \frac{\gamma}{\mu}\vartheta(1-\beta)[\phi[\omega_0 - (1-\beta)b_s^*] - (\omega_0 - b_s^*)] \tag{6.24}$$

Expected inflation can be defined as

$$\mathbb{E}\pi = p\pi^H + (1-p)\pi^L = p[\pi^L - \frac{\gamma}{\mu}\vartheta(1-\beta)[\phi[\omega_0 - (1-\beta)b_s^*] -$$
$$-(\omega_0 - b_s^*)]] + (1-p)\pi^L =$$
$$= \frac{\gamma}{\mu}\lambda\phi[\omega_0 - (1-\beta)b_s^*] - p\frac{\gamma}{\mu}\vartheta(1-\beta)[\phi[\omega_0 - (1-\beta)b_s^*] -$$
$$-(\omega_0 - b_s^*)] \tag{6.25}$$

The nominal interest rate on domestic public bonds, r, defined implicitly yields:

By applying Fisher equation $p(1+r-\gamma\pi^H)+(1-p)(1+r-\gamma\pi^L)=$ $=1+r^*$, we get

$$r=r^*+\frac{\gamma^2}{\mu}\phi\lambda[\omega_0-(1-\beta)b_s^*]-\gamma^2\frac{p}{\mu}\vartheta(1-\beta)[\phi[\omega_0-(1-\beta)b_s^*]- -(\omega_0-b_s^*)] \tag{6.26}$$

The government's optimization problem with respect of the share of nominal debtholdings, ϕ of banks, takes the form:

$$\max_{\varphi} \mathbb{E}C=\mathbb{E}Y-\frac{1}{2}\mu\mathbb{E}\pi^2-\lambda\mathbb{E}T$$

Expected total output of the economy, $\mathbb{E}Y$, is defined on equation (6.20) basis, using the expressions for π and r from equations (6.24) and (6.26) respectively:

$$\mathbb{E}Y=W_1+p\vartheta\beta\omega_{1b}+p(1-p)\frac{\gamma^2}{\mu}\vartheta^2(1-\beta)^2[\phi(\omega_0-(1-\beta)b_s^*)- -(\omega_0-b_s^*)]^2-p\vartheta(1+r^*)\beta b_f^*-(1+r^*)b_f^* \tag{6.30}$$

By deriving the expected total output of the domestic economy, with respect to ϕ, yields:

$$\frac{\partial\mathbb{E}Y}{\partial\phi}=2p(1-p)\frac{\gamma^2}{\mu}\vartheta^2(1-\beta)^2[\phi(\omega_0-(1-\beta)b_s^*)-(\omega_0- -b_s^*)][(\omega_0-(1-\beta)b_s^*)] \tag{6.31}$$

where, $\omega_0-(1-\beta)b_s^*=\beta b_b>0$ defines total bonds held by banks.

a) In case $\phi(\omega_0-(1-\beta)b_s^*)<\omega_0-b_s^*$, i.e. for $\phi\rightarrow 0$ (the amount of nominal bonds are small), the sign of the derivative in (6.31) indicates that inflation favors the banks and total output of the economy, $\mathbb{E}Y$ decreases with ϕ.

b) In case $\phi(\omega_0-(1-\beta)b_s^*)>\omega_0-b_s^*$, i.e. nominal bonds are greater than deposits, an increase in ϕ, also increases total output of the economy, $\mathbb{E}Y$.

Rewrite (6.31) as

$$\frac{\partial \mathbb{E}Y}{\partial \phi} = 2p(1-p)\frac{\gamma^2}{\mu}\vartheta^2(1-\beta)^2[\phi\beta b_b - (\omega_0 - b_s^*)]\,\beta b_b \qquad (6.32)$$

Expected inflation is given by $\mathbb{E}\pi^2 = p\pi^{H2} + (1-p)\pi^{L2}$
where $\pi^L = \frac{\gamma}{\mu}\lambda\phi[\omega_0 - (1-\beta)b_s^*] = \frac{\gamma}{\mu}\lambda\phi\beta b_b$ (6.33)
and,

$$\pi^H = \frac{\gamma}{\mu}\lambda\phi[\omega_0 - (1-\beta)b_s^*] - \frac{\gamma}{\mu}\vartheta(1-\beta)[\phi[\omega_0 - (1-\beta)b_s^*] - $$
$$-(\omega_0 - b_s^*)] = \frac{\gamma}{\mu}\lambda\phi\beta b_b - \frac{\gamma}{\mu}\vartheta(1-\beta)[\phi\beta b_b - (\omega_0 - b_s^*)] \qquad (6.34)$$

Consequently,

$$\mathbb{E}\pi^2 = p\{\frac{\gamma}{\mu}\lambda\phi\beta b_b - \frac{\gamma}{\mu}\vartheta(1-\beta)[\phi\beta b_b - (\omega_0 - b_s^*)]\}^2 + (1 - $$
$$-p)(\frac{\gamma}{\mu}\lambda\phi\beta b_b)^2 \qquad (6.35^1)$$

By deriving the term of expected inflation (second term in maximization problem), with respect of ϕ, yields:

$$\frac{\partial}{\partial \phi}(\frac{1}{2}\mu\mathbb{E}\pi^2) = \frac{\gamma^2}{\mu}p\beta b_b\{\lambda - \vartheta(1-\beta)\}\{\phi\lambda\beta b_b - \vartheta(1-\beta)[\phi\beta b_b - $$
$$-(\omega_0 - b_s^*)]\} + (1-p)\frac{\gamma^2}{\mu}\phi\lambda^2\beta^2 b_b^2 \qquad (6.35^2)$$

While, by deriving the term of expected taxes (third term in maximization problem), with respect of ϕ, yields

$$\lambda\frac{\partial \mathbb{E}T}{\partial \phi} = 0 \qquad (6.36)$$

Finally, the first-order condition of the government optimization problem with respect of ϕ, results:

$$\frac{\partial \mathbb{E}C}{\partial \phi} = \underbrace{2p(1-p)\vartheta^2(1-\beta)^2[\phi\beta b_b - (\omega_0 - b_s^*)]}_{\text{Distribution effect}} - p\{\lambda - $$
$$-\vartheta(1-\beta\}\{\underbrace{\phi\lambda\beta b_b}_{\pi^H \text{ effect}} - $$
$$-\underbrace{\vartheta(1-\beta)[\phi\beta b_b - (\omega_0 - b_s^*)]\}}_{\pi^H \text{ effect}} - (1-p)\phi\lambda^2\beta b_b \qquad (6.37)$$

We can rewrite equation (6.37) as a combination of (d, K, λ), such that

$$d = \omega_0 - b_s^*$$
$$K = \vartheta(1 - \beta)$$

and λ is a marginal cost of taxation. As a result, (6.37) takes the form:
$$\frac{\partial \mathbb{E}C}{\partial \phi} = [(1-2p)pK^2 + 2pK\lambda - \lambda^2]\phi\beta b_b - [(1-2p)K + \lambda]pKd$$

for simplicity, define as

$$\alpha = (1-2p)pK^2 + 2pK\lambda - \lambda^2$$
$$\beta = (1-2p)K + \lambda$$

Proof: The cases to consider that can impact the equilibrium are as follows

Case 1. $\beta > 0$ and $\alpha > 0$:
$\beta = (1-2p)K + \lambda > 0$ always if $p \leq \frac{1}{2}$

if instead $p > \frac{1}{2}$, for having $\beta > 0$ it should be $\lambda > (1-2p)K$, which implies $\lambda > K$.

while, $\alpha > 0$ implies $(1-2p)pK^2 + 2pK\lambda - \lambda^2 > 0$

$$\lambda^2 - 2pK\lambda - (1-2p)pK^2 < 0 \rightarrow$$
$$\lambda = pK \pm \sqrt{p^2K^2 + (1-2p)pK^2}$$

As a result, λ should belong to the interval: $K[p - \sqrt{p(1-p)}] < \lambda < K[p+ + \sqrt{p(1-p)}]$

To summarize this case:

for $\alpha > 0$, it should be $K[p - \sqrt{p(1-p)}] < \lambda < K[p + \sqrt{p(1-p)}]$
for $\beta > 0$ and $p > \frac{1}{2}$, it should be $\lambda > (2p-1)K$
for $\beta > 0$ and $p \leq \frac{1}{2}$, it always holds

Hence, to have $\alpha > 0$ and $\beta > 0$, with $p > \frac{1}{2}$, we need $(2p-1)K < \lambda <$ $< K[p + \sqrt{p(1-p)}]$, which implies that λ must be high but not too much to allow a small share of nominal domestic debt. While, to have $\alpha > 0$ and $\beta > 0$, with $p \leq \frac{1}{2}$, we need $K[p - \sqrt{p(1-p)}] < \lambda < K[p + \sqrt{p(1-p)}]$.

Case 2. $\beta > 0$ and $\alpha < 0$:

$\beta = (1-2p)K + \lambda > 0$ always if $p \leq \frac{1}{2}$

if instead $p > \frac{1}{2}$, for having $\beta > 0$ it should be $\lambda > (1-2p)K$, which implies $\lambda > K$.

while, $\alpha < 0$ implies $(1-2p)pK^2 + 2pK\lambda - \lambda^2 < 0$

$$\lambda^2 - 2pK\lambda - (1-2p)pK^2 > 0 \rightarrow$$
$$\lambda = pK \pm \sqrt{p^2K^2 + (1-2p)pK^2}$$

As a result, λ should belong to the interval: $\lambda < K[p - \sqrt{p(1-p)}]$ and $\lambda > K[p + \sqrt{p(1-p)}]$

To summarize this case:

for $\alpha < 0$, it should be $\lambda < K[p - \sqrt{p(1-p)}]$ and $\lambda > K[p + \sqrt{p(1-p)}]$
for $\beta > 0$ and $p > \frac{1}{2}$ it should be $\lambda > (1-2p)K$
for $\beta > 0$ and $p \leq \frac{1}{2}$ it always holds

Hence, to have $\alpha < 0$ and $\beta > 0$ with $p > \frac{1}{2}$, we need $\lambda > K[p +$ $+\sqrt{p(1-p)}]$, which implies that for high λ the share of nominal domestic debt $\phi = 0$. While, to have $\alpha < 0$ and $\beta > 0$ with $p \leq \frac{1}{2}$, we need $\lambda < K[p -$ $-\sqrt{p(1-p)}]$ and $\lambda > K[p + \sqrt{p(1-p)}]$.

Case 3. $\beta < 0$ and $\alpha > 0$:
$\beta = (1-2p)K + \lambda < 0$ never holds if $p \leq \frac{1}{2}$

We are left with the case $p > \frac{1}{2}$: for $\beta < 0$ it should be $\lambda < (1-2p)K$.

While, $\alpha > 0$ implies $(1-2p)pK^2 + 2pK\lambda - \lambda^2 > 0$, and

As a result, λ should belong to the interval: $K[p - \sqrt{p(1-p)}] < \lambda < K[p+ + \sqrt{p(1-p)}]$

To summarize this case:

for $\alpha > 0$, it should be $K[p - \sqrt{p(1-p)}] < \lambda < K[p + \sqrt{p(1-p)}]$
for $\beta < 0$ and $p > \frac{1}{2}$, it should be $\lambda < (1-2p)K$

Hence, to have $\alpha > 0$ and $\beta < 0$ with $p > \frac{1}{2}$, we need $K[p - \sqrt{p(1-p)}] < < \lambda < K[p + \sqrt{p(1-p)}$, which implies that for high p, low λ and high K, the share of domestic debt $\phi = 1$..

Case 4. $\beta < 0$ and $\alpha < 0$:

$\beta = (1-2p)K + \lambda < 0$ never holds if $p \leq \frac{1}{2}$

As in previous case, we are left with $p > \frac{1}{2}$: for $\beta < 0$ it should be $\lambda < (1-2p)K$.

While, $\alpha < 0$ implies $(1-2p)pK^2 + 2pK\lambda - \lambda^2 < 0$, and

As a result, λ should belong to the interval: $\lambda < K[p - \sqrt{p(1-p)}]$ and $\lambda > K[p + \sqrt{p(1-p)}]$

To summarize this case:

for $\alpha < 0$, it should be $\lambda < K[p - \sqrt{p(1-p)}]$ and $\lambda > K[p + \sqrt{p(1-p)}]$
for $\beta < 0$ and $p > \frac{1}{2}$, it should be $\lambda < (1-2p)K$

Hence, to have $\alpha < 0$ and $\beta < 0$ with $p > \frac{1}{2}$, we need $\lambda < K[p - -\sqrt{p(1-p)}]$.

We can summarize all 4 cases with respect to the level of λ:

If probability of high state of productivity is high, $p > \frac{1}{2}$:

The smallest value of λ (case 3: $K\left[p - \sqrt{p(1-p)}\right] < \lambda < (2p-1)K$, $\alpha > 0$, $\beta < 0$, which means high p, low λ and high K; case 4: $\lambda < K[p -$

$-\sqrt{p(1-p)}]$, $\alpha < 0$, $\beta < 0$) is related to the highest share of nominal domestic debt in total banks debtholding $\phi = 1$;

The highest value of λ (case 2: $\lambda > K[p + \sqrt{p(1-p)}]$, $\alpha < 0$, $\beta > 0$) is related to the $\phi = 0$ share of nominal domestic debt in total banks debtholding.

We can check the difference between expected consumptions in two extreme cases:

$\mathbb{E}C(\phi = 1)$ and $\mathbb{E}C(\phi = 0)$, when λ takes the intermediate value, specifically in the case 1, where:

$(2p-1)K < \lambda < K[p + \sqrt{p(1-p)}]$, $\alpha > 0$ and $\beta > 0$.

Recall:

$$\mathbb{E}C_{\phi=1} = \mathbb{E}Y_{\phi=1} - \frac{1}{2}\mu\mathbb{E}\pi^2_{\phi=1} - \lambda\mathbb{E}T_{\phi=1}$$
$$\mathbb{E}C_{\phi=0} = \mathbb{E}Y_{\phi=0} - \frac{1}{2}\mu\mathbb{E}\pi^2_{\phi=0} - \lambda\mathbb{E}T_{\phi=0}$$

where $\mathbb{E}Y, \mathbb{E}\pi^2$ and $\mathbb{E}T$ are defined from (6.30), (6.35[1]) and (6.22) respectively.

Check the difference between $\mathbb{E}C_{\phi=1}$ and $\mathbb{E}C_{\phi=0}$:

$$\mathbb{E}C_{\phi=1} - \mathbb{E}C_{\phi=0} = p(1-p)\frac{\gamma^2}{\mu}K^2[\beta b_b - d]^2 - \frac{1}{2}\frac{\gamma^2}{\mu}p\{\lambda\beta b_b - -K[\beta b_b - d]\}^2 - -\frac{1}{2}(1-p)\frac{\gamma^2}{\mu}(\lambda^2(\beta b_b)^2 - p(1-p)\frac{\gamma^2}{\mu}K^2 d^2 + \frac{1}{2}\frac{\gamma^2}{\mu}pK^2 d^2 \quad (6.38^1)$$

It is straightforward to prove that equation (6.38[1]) reduces to

$$\mathbb{E}C_{\phi=1} - \mathbb{E}C_{\phi=0} = -[\lambda - (2p-1)K][\lambda\beta b_b + 2pKd] + K\beta b_b[\lambda - -(2p-1)pK] \quad (6.38^2)$$

Now we check the sign of (6.38[2]). Recall, we are assessing the case, when λ belongs to the interval: $(2p-1)K < \lambda < K[p + \sqrt{p(1-p)}]$ and $p > \frac{1}{2}$. Under this setting:

1st term of (6.38²): $-[\lambda-(2p-1)K][\lambda\beta b_b+2pKd]<0$, since $\lambda-$ $-(2p-1)K>0$

2nd term of (6.38²): $K\beta b_b[\lambda-(2p-1)pK]>0$, since:

$$\lambda-(2p-1)pK=\lambda-(2p-1)K+(2p-1)K-(2p-1)pK=$$
$$=\underbrace{\lambda-(2p-1)K}_{>0}+\underbrace{(2p-1)K(1-p)}_{>0}>0$$

To define the sign of the difference: $\mathbb{E}C_{\phi=1}-\mathbb{E}C_{\phi=0}$, we look for the cases as follows

if λ is close to lower bound, i.e. $\lambda\approx(2p-1)K$, the difference: $\mathbb{E}C_{\phi=1}-\mathbb{E}C_{\phi=0}>0$, which implies that $\phi=1$ is optimal.

if λ is close to upper bound, i.e. $\lambda\approx K[p+\sqrt{p(1-p)}]$, we have:

$$\mathbb{E}C_{\phi=1}-\mathbb{E}C_{\phi=0}=-\big[K[p+\sqrt{p(1-p)}]-(2p-1)K\big][\lambda\beta b_b+$$
$$+2pKd]+K\beta b_b[K[p+\sqrt{p(1-p)}]-(2p-1)pK]\rightarrow$$
$$\mathbb{E}C_{\phi=1}-\mathbb{E}C_{\phi=0}=-\big[\sqrt{p(1-p)}]+1-p\big][\lambda\beta b_b+2pKd]+$$
$$+K\beta b_b[\sqrt{p(1-p)}]+2p(1-p)] \qquad (6.38^3)$$

the sign of (6.38³) is defined by the sign of the following polynomial: $-[\lambda\beta b_b+2pKd]+K\beta b_b$. This term is negative whenever $\lambda>K$. Hence, $\mathbb{E}C_{\phi=1}-\mathbb{E}C_{\phi=0}<0$, which implies that $\phi=1$ is optimal.

REFERENCES

Abbas S.M. Ali and Christiansen Jakob E. (2007), The Role of Domestic Debt Markets in Economic Growth: An Empirical Investigation for Low Income Countries and Emerging Markets. *IMF Working Paper, WP/07/127.*

Acemoglu D., Johnson S., and Robinson J. (2000), The Colonial Origins of Comparative Development: An Empirical Investigation. *mimeo, MIT.*

Alesina A. and Gatti R. (1995), Independent central banks: low inflation at no cost? *American Economic Review,* 196-200.

Allen F., Bartiloro L., Kowalevski O. (2006), Does Economic structure Determine Financial Structure? *mimeo.*

Allen F., Borensztein E., Yeyati E., Panizza U. Living with Debt, Economic and Social Progress in Latin America. *2007 Report.*

Ananiashvili I. and Papava V. (2012), Taxes, Production Technology, and Economic Growth, *Problems of Economic Transition, vol. 54, no. 12,* 71–91.

Aspromourgos T., Rees D., White G. (2010), Public Debt Sustainability and Alternative Theories of Interest. *Cambridge Journal of Economics, 34,* 433-477.

Back J.L., Musgrave, R.A. (1941), A stable purchasing power bond. *American Economic Review, 31*, 823-825.

Baldacci E., Kumar M.(2010), Fiscal Deficits, Public Debt and Sovereign Bond Yields. *IMF Working Paper, WP/10/184.*

Barro R. and Gordon D. (1983a), A positive theory of monetary policy in a natural rate model. *Journal of Political Economy*, 589-610.

Barro R. and Gordon D. (1983b), Rules, discretion, and reputation in a model of monetary policy. *Journal of Monetary Economics*, 101-120.

Barro R.(1979), On the Determinants of the Public Debt. *Journal of Political Economy, Vol. 85 (5),* 940-71.

Barro, R. (1995), Inflation and Economic Growth, *NBER WP No.5326.*

Bartiloro L., Kowalevski O.(2006), Does Economic Structure Determine Financial Structure? *Mimeo.*

Beck T., A. damirgüc-Kunt and R. Levine (2003), Law, Endowments, and Finance. *Journal of Financial Economics, Vol.70(2),* 137-181.

Beetsma R.M.W.J., Bovenberg A.L. (1997), Central bank independence and public debt policy. *Journal of Economics Dynamics and Control, 21 (4-5),* 873-894.

Bencivenga V.R. and Smith B.D. (1992), Some unpleasant Supply Side Arithmetic. *Journal of Monetary Economics,* 507-24.

Berg A., Borenztein E., Sahay R., and Zettelmeyer J. (1999), The Evolution of Output in Transition Economies: Explaining the Differences. *IMF Working Paper , WP/99/73.*

Bhide A.(1993), The hidden Costs of Stock Market Liquidity. *Journal of Financial Economics, 34,* 31-51.

Blundell R. and Bond S. (1998), Initial Conditions and Moment Restrictions in Dynamic Panel Data Models. *Journal of Econometrics, Vol.87(1),* 115-43.

Boynd J.H., Levine R., Smith B.D. (2001), The Impact of Inflation on Financial Sector Performance, *Journal of Monetary Economics, V.47(2),* 221-248.

Burnside C., M. Eichenbaum, and S. Rebelo, 2001, Prospective Deficits and the Asian Currency Crisis, *Journal of Political Economy, Vol. 109 (6),* 1155-97.

Caballero R.J., Krishnamurthy A.(2004), *Fiscal Policy and Financial Depth.* Working Paper, no. 10532. National Bureau of Economic Research, Cambridge, MA.

Calvo G.A. (1988), Servicing the public debt: The role of expectations. *American Economic Review 78(4),* 647-661.

Chari V. V., Kehoe P.J. and Prescott E. C. (1989), Time consistency and policy. In R. Barro (ed.), Modern Business Cycle Theory. Harvard University Press, Cambridge (MA), 265-305.

Checherita C. and Rother P.(2010), The Impact of High and Growing Government Debt on Economic Growth An Empirical Investigation for the Euro Area. *European Central Bank, WP no. 1237.*

Chinn M. D. and Ito H. (2006), What Matters for Financial Development? Capital Controls, Institutions, and Interactions. *Journal of Development Economics, 81(1),* 163-192.

Cordella T., Ricci L.A. and Ruiz-Arranz M.(2005), Debt overhang or Debt irrelevance? Revisiting the Debt-Growth link. *IMF Working paper WP/05/223.*

Cukierman A. (1994), Commitment through delegation, political influence and central bank independence. In de-Beaufort-Wijnholds, J.O. et al. (Eds.), A Framework for Monetary Stability, Financial and Monetary Policy Studies, Vol. 27. Kluwer Academics, Dordrecht, Boston, 55-74.

De Melo M., Denizer C., and Gelb A. (1996), Patterns of Transition from Plan to Market. *World Bank Economic Review, Vol.10 (September).*

DemirgüÇ-Kunt A. and R. Levine (2001), Financial Structure and Economic Growth. The MIT Press.

Dotsey M.(1994), Some unpleasant Supply Side Arithmetic. *Journal of Monetary Economics,* 507-24.

Easterly W. and Levine R. (2003), Tropics, Germs, and Crops: How Endowments influence Economic Development. *Journal of Monetary Economics, 50,* 3-39.

Elbadawi et al (1997), Debt Overhang and Economic Growth in Sub-Saharan Africa. In External Finance for Low-Income Countries, Washington DC.: IMF Institute Ch.5.

Ergungor O.(2004), Market vs. Bank-Based Financial Systems: Do Rights and Regulations Really Matter?, *Journal of Banking and Finance 28(12),* 2869-2887.

Falcetti E., Missale A. (2001), Public debt indexation and denomination with an independent central bank. *European Economic Review, 46 (2002),* 1825-1859.

Fischer S., Sahay R. (1996b), Economies in Transition: The Beginning of Growth. *American Economic Review, Vol.86 (May).*

Fischer S., Sahay R. (2000), The Transition Economies After Ten Years. IMF report.

Fischer S., Sahay R. (2004), Transition Economies: The Role of Institutions and Initial Conditions. Calvo Conference, April 2004.

Fischer S., Sahay R., Vègh A. (1996a), Stabilization and Growth in Transition Economies: The early experience. *Journal of Economic Perspectives, Vol.10 (Spring).*

Futagami K., Hori T., Ohdoi R. (2010), Debt Policy and Economic Growth in a Small Open Economy Model with Productive Government Spending. *ADBI Working Paper Series, No. 212.*

Gale W. and Orszag P. (2003), The Economic Effects of Long-term Fiscal Discipline. Urban-Brookings Tax Policy Center Discussion Paper No.8 (Washington: Brookings Institution).

Gelos R., Sahay R. (2000), Financial Market Spillovers in Transition Economies. *IMF Working Paper, WP/00/71.*

Gennaioli N., Martin A. and Rossi S. (2010), Sovereign Default, Domestic Banks and Financial Institutions. *Centre for Economic Policy Research, Discussion Paper No.7955.*

Greenwood J. and Jovanovic B. (1990), Financial Development, Growth, and the Distribution of Income. *Journal of Political Economy, 98,* 1076-1107.

Guiso L., Sapienza P. and Zingales P. (2004), The Role of Social Capital in Financial Development. *American Economic review, 94,* 526-556.

Guscina A. (2008), Impact of Macroeconomic, Political, and Institutional Factors on the Structure of Government Debt in Emerging market Countries. *IMF Working Paper, WP/08/205.*

Haber S. H. (2004), Political Competition and Economic growth: Lessons from the Political Economy of Bank Regulation in the United States and Mexico. Stanford University, *mimeo.*

Haber S.H., Mayer N. and Razo A. (2003), The Politics of Property Rights: Political Instability, Credible Commitments, and Economic Growth in Mexico. Cambridge University Press.

Harrabi et al (2007), Debt Relief and Credit to the Private Sector in African Countries, *African Development Review, 19(3),* 469-480.

Hauner D. (2008), Public Debt and financial development, *Journal of Development Economics, Vol.88(2),* 171-1170.

Helbling T., Mody A., and Sahay R.(2004), Debt Accumulation in the CIS-7 Countries: Bad luck, Bad Policies, or Bad Advice? *IMF Working Paper, WP/04/93.*

Hemming R., M. Kell, and A. Schimmelpfenning (2003), Fiscal Vulnerability and Financial Crises in Emerging Market Economies, *IMF Occasional Paper, No.218.*

Holmstrom, B. and Tirole L. (1993), Market Liquidity and Performance Monitoring. *Journal of Political Economy, 101,* 678-709.

Huang Y. and Temple J. (2005 (July)), Does External Trade Promote Financial Development? *Discussion Paper 05/575,* University of Bristol.

Huybens E., Smith B.D. (1999), Inflation, financial markets and long-run real activity. *Journal of Monetary Economics, 43,* 283-315.

Imbs J. and Ranciere R. (2005), The Overhang Hangover, *World Bank WP, n.3673,* August 2005.

Irons J. and Bivens J. (2010), Government Debt and Economic Growth. *EPI Briefing Paper, n.271.*

Jeanne O. and Guscina A. (2006), Government Debt in Emerging Market Countries: A New Data set. *IMF Working Paper, WP/06/98.*

King R.G. and Levine R. (1993), Finance and growth: Schumpeter might be right. *Quarterly Journal of Economics, 108,* 717-737.

Krugman, P. (1988), Financing vs. forgiving a debt overhang, *Journal of development Economics, 29(2),* 407-437.

Kumar, M. and J. Woo (2010), Public Debt and Growth, *IMF Working Paper, WP 10/174.*

La Porta R., Lopez-de-Silanes F., Shleifer A., and Vishny R.W. (1998), Law and Finance. *Journal of Political Economy, 106,* 1113-1155.

Levine R. (1991), Stock markets, Growth, and Tax Policy. *Journal of Finance, 46,* 1445-1465.

Levine R. (1996), Financial Development and Economic Growth: Views and Agenda. *WB Policy Research Working Paper, No. 1678.*

Levine R. (2003), More on Finance and Growth: More Finance, More Growth? *Federal Reserve Bank of St. Luis Review, Vol.85, 31-46.*

Levine R. (2005), Finance and Growth: Theory and Evidence in P. Aghion and S.N. Durlauf(eds) *Handbook of Economic Growth*, North-Holland.

Levine R.(1999), Law, Finance, and Economic Growth, *Journal of Financial Intermediation, 8,* 36-67.

Levine R., Loyaza N., and Beck T. (1999), Financial Intermediation and Growth: Causality and Causes. *WB Policy Research Working Paper, No. 2059.*

Lucas R. E., Stokey N., (1983), Optimal fiscal and monetary policy in an economy without capital. *Journal of Monetary Economics, 12,* 55-93.

Mayer C., and Sussman O. (2001), The assessment: finance, law and growth. *Oxford Review of Economic Policy, 17(4),* 457-66.

McCallum B. (1997), Crucial issues concerning central bank independence. *Journal of Monetary Economics,* 99-112.

McKinnon R.(1973), Money and Capital in Economic Development. Washington, DC, The Brooking Institution.

Missale A. and Blanchard O. J. (1991), The Debt Burden and Debt Maturity. *NBER WP 3394,* 1991.

Modigliani F. (1961), Long-run Implications of Alternative Fiscal Policies and The Burden of The National Debt. *Economic Journal, 71 (284),* 730-755.

Pattilo C., H. Poirson and L. Ricci (2002), External Debt and Growth. *IMF Working Paper, WP/02/69.*

Piga G. (2000), Dependent and accountable: Evidence From the Modern Theory of Central Banking. *Journal of Economic Surveys, Vol.14,* No.5.

Presbitero A. (2006), The Debt-Growth Nexus: A Dynamic Panel Data Estimation. Rivista Italiana degli Economisti, a.XI, n.3, Decembre 2006.

Presbitero A. (2010), Total Public Debt and Economic Growth in Developing Countries. Working Paper Series, http://ssrn.com/abstract=1697506.

Presbitero A.(2008), The Debt-Growth Nexus in Poor Countries: A Reassessment. *Economics: The Open-Access,Open-Assessment E-Journal, Vol. 2,* 2008-30. doi:10.5018/economics-ejournal.ja.2008-30.

Quy-Toan Do and Levchenko A.(2004), Trade and Financial Development. *World Bank WP*, Vol.3347.

Rajan R.G. and Zingales (1998), Financial Dependence and Growth. *American Economic Review, 88,* 559-86.

Rajan R.G. and Zingales L. (2003), The Great Reversals: The Politics of Financial Development in the Twentieth Century. *Journal of Financial Economics, 69,* 5-50.

Reinhart C.M. and Rogoff K.S. (2010 a), Growth in a time of debt. *NBER WP 15639.*

Reinhart C.M. and Rogoff K.S.(2010 b), From Financial crash to debt crisis. *NBER WP 15795.*

Robinson J. (1952), The Generalization of the General Theory. In *the Rate of interest and other Essays,* London: MacMillan.

Rogoff K. (1985), The optimal degree of commitment to an intermediate monetary target. *Quarterly Journal of Economics 100,* 1169-1190.

Roodman d. (2006 (December)), How to do xtabond2: An Introduction to "Difference" and "System" GMM in STATA. WP 103, Center for Global Development.

Roubini N. and X. Sala-i-Martin (1992), Financial Repression and Economic Growth. *Journal of Development Economics, 39,* 5-30.

Roubini N. and X. Sala-i-Martin (1995), A Growth Model of Inflation, Tax Evasion, and Financial Repression. *Journal of Monetary Economics, 35,* 275-301.

Schclarek A. (2004), Debt and Economic Growth in Developing and Industrial Countries. *mimeo.*

Stulz R.M. and R. Williamson (2003), Culture, Openness, and Finance. *Journal of Financial Economics, 70,* 313-349.

Walsh C.E. (1998), Optimal Contracts for Central Bankers. *American Economic Review,* 150-167.

INDEX

D

E

F

G

H

I

J

K

L

M

N

O

P

R

S

T